THE REEVE'S PROLOGUE
AND TALE

Miller + Reve together against
Clerks, 238

Miller attempts to increase
clerks
270

Individualisation of Scholars   83

Miller only concerned about Rank
418

A MILLER DEPICTED IN THE
LUTTRELL PSALTER
The British Library.

THE

REEVE'S PROLOGUE & TALE
WITH THE
COOK'S PROLOGUE
AND THE
FRAGMENT OF HIS TALE

FROM THE CANTERBURY TALES

BY

GEOFFREY CHAUCER

Edited with Introduction, Notes
and Glossary by
A. C. SPEARING and J. E. SPEARING

CAMBRIDGE
UNIVERSITY PRESS

PUBLISHED BY THE PRESS SYNDICATE OF THE UNIVERSITY OF CAMBRIDGE
The Pitt Building, Trumpington Street, Cambridge, United Kingdom

CAMBRIDGE UNIVERSITY PRESS
The Edinburgh Building, Cambridge CB2 2RU, UK   http://www.cup.cam.ac.uk
40 West 20th Street, New York, NY 10011–4211, USA   http://www.cup.org
10 Stamford Road, Oakleigh, Melbourne 3166, Australia
Ruiz de Alarcón 13, 28014 Madrid, Spain

First published 1979
Eighth printing 1999

Printed in the United Kingdom at the University Press, Cambridge

Typeface Imprint

A catalogue record for this book is available from the British Library

Library of Congress Cataloguing in Publication data
Chaucer, Geoffrey, d. 1400.
The reeve's prologue and tale with The cook's
prologue and the fragment of the The cook's tale from
the Canterbury tales.
(Selected tales from Chaucer)
In Middle English.
Includes bibliographical references.

I. Spearing, A. C. II. Spearing, J. E.
III. Chaucer, Geoffrey, d. 1400. Canterbury tales.
The cook's tale. 1979. IV. Title.
PR1868.R42S6   1979   821'.1   78–18695

ISBN 0 521 22211 7 paperback

CONTENTS

NOTE ON THE FRONTISPIECE

This illustration is taken from the Luttrell Psalter (British Library MS Add. 42130), an East Anglian manuscript of about 1340. It shows an ape-like grasping miller, conforming to the medieval stereotype discussed in the Introduction, pp. 37ff. He is about to place a sack of flour on the back of one of his customers, for her to carry it away. Attached to his belt is a wooden shovel, for measuring out flour and grain. Like Chaucer's Simkin, this miller is grossly caricatured for the benefit of an upper-class public, for the psalter was created for Sir Geoffrey Luttrell, a wealthy East Anglian knight. Though the manuscript is from the right century and the right part of England for *The Reeve's Tale*, the mill is driven here by wind, not water.

PREFACE

In preparing this, the first separate edition of either *The Reeve's Prologue and Tale* or *The Cook's Prologue and Tale*, our greatest debt has been to Professor J. A. W. Bennett's *Chaucer at Oxford and at Cambridge*, a learned and entertaining book which is a major source of new information about *The Reeve's Tale* and its setting. We hope that this general acknowledgement will stand in place of the many specific references that would otherwise be necessary. We have also been influenced, inevitably, by many of the other studies listed in the Suggestions for Further Reading (p. 114), and especially by Murray Copland's article, 'The *Reeve's Tale* – Harlotrie or Sermonyng?', a most distinguished piece of criticism.

Our gratitude is due to Form 6Y (1977–78) of Long Road Sixth Form College, Cambridge – situated, appropriately enough, less than two miles from the scene of *The Reeve's Tale* – for allowing the notes and glossary of this edition to be tested on them before publication, and for making a number of helpful suggestions. We are grateful, too, to our daughter Cassandra for her help with the proofs.

A.C.S.
J.E.S.

CAMBRIDGE
January, 1978

INTRODUCTION

In more than one way, *The Reeve's Tale* has a low reputation. Certainly, someone who had not read it would gain little encouragement to do so from what has been written about it by most of the comparatively few scholars and critics who have discussed it. We do not have to go back to the days of Dr Bowdler and his expurgated Shakespeare to find one scholar describing *The Reeve's Tale* with disgust as the product of its teller's 'sewer of a mind', another dismissing it as one of the 'most limited and least valuable' of Chaucer's tales, or a third, very recent writer categorizing it as 'disgusting,...repellent,...enervated salaciousness'. Even those who have praised it have tended to do so in terms that make it seem remarkably unattractive. The author of what is perhaps the most penetrating single study of it ends by defining it as 'a grey tale for grey and depressing people'; and it is difficult to feel much eagerness to read it when another distinguished critic praises its 'rendering of a particularly bilious view of life'. A favourite device is to compare *The Reeve's Tale* to its disadvantage with its predecessor and twin in *The Canterbury Tales*, *The Miller's Tale*. The scholar from whom we have learned most about the social setting of *The Reeve's Tale* nevertheless assesses it as 'cruder and...coarser' than *The Miller's Tale*; the author of a survey of Chaucer's work wearily observes that '*The Reeve's Tale* is clever enough, but its lacks the variety of *The Miller's Tale*'; and another recent writer tells us that 'The wholesome sexuality of the Miller's Tale is replaced in the Reeve's by theft, mistrust, and plain malevolence.'

Such is the power of a critical consensus that for a long time we vaguely acquiesced in this devaluation of *The Reeve's Tale*, somehow managing to forget that each time we actually read it we found it extremely funny. It was only after some delay that doubts made themselves felt, and especially about that conventional unfavourable comparison with *The Miller's Tale*. 'Wholesome sexuality'? An odd way, perhaps, to describe the cuckolding and public ridicule of a harmless old man, accompanied by a kiss directed to the behind of the beloved and the scalding of the lover's behind with a red-hot coulter, applied so vigorously that 'Of gooth the skin an hande-brede aboute'. In *The Reeve's Tale*, no events so physically repellent take place, nor is there any such encouragement to visualize horrors; and the chief sufferer, the proud and grasping miller, thoroughly deserves what he gets.

In artistry, too, *The Reeve's Tale* has some important points of superiority over its predecessor. If it has less variety, it is surely more satisfyingly integrated. For one thing, the world of everyday work, which, as we shall see, is the normal setting of Chaucer's comic tales, is here made more fully significant, for Simkin's profession as miller is far more central to the meaning of *The Reeve's Tale* than is John's as carpenter to that of *The Miller's Tale*. For another, the characteristics of the teller play a larger part in *The Reeve's Tale* than in the Miller's: the Reeve's interest in horses, for instance, leads to a central theme of his story, while the boorish and drunken Miller seems in many ways a

2

most unlikely mouthpiece for the almost perversely fantastic ingenuity of *The Miller's Tale*. Again, *The Reeve's Tale* moves further than the Miller's – further perhaps than any other poem of Chaucer's – towards a consistent realism of character, motive, and social and economic setting; and its special interest, as being the first work in English to use local dialect as a means of characterization, is only one aspect of this realism.

But we neither need nor wish to devalue *The Miller's Tale* in order to revalue the Reeve's. Both are outstanding examples of Chaucer's mature art in the last decade of his life. Both are hilariously funny, both are delightfully improper; both are at the same time imaginative achievements of lasting value. It is here that our chief difficulty may come in discussing and assessing both tales. We are not used to talking about poems or other works of art in terms that will allow them to be at the same time funny and important. The difficulty existed in Chaucer's time and for Chaucer himself: the distinction drawn between *ernest* and *game* in the final lines of the Prologue to *The Miller's Tale* – 'And eek men shal nat maken ernest of game' – cannot help implying that *game* can escape reproof only by admitting that it is merely trivial. Yet in the Middle Ages, the comic was admitted as at least part of the most important art, in the form of gargoyles and carved misericords in cathedrals or of grotesques in the margins of devotional books. In *The Canterbury Tales*, however, the comic is more than marginal. In our time, despite the essentially comic nature of such twentieth-century masterpieces as James Joyce's

Ulysses, the growing seriousness of academic English studies has made it still more difficult to acknowledge that the greatness of a literary work may exist not behind or despite its power to make us laugh but in that power: in its lively pace, its perfect timing, its perception of incongruity, its ability to relieve us for the moment of the burdens of inhibition and moral responsibility. In *The Reeve's Tale*, and in medieval comic tales generally, there is a streak of callousness that may at first shock twentieth-century readers, whose tastes are likely to have been formed by a tradition of writing and a social ethos in which tolerance, sympathy and forgiveness are key values; though they will not surprise those who have enjoyed the work of such major post-medieval comic writers as Ben Jonson, Jonathan Swift, or Vladimir Nabokov. If there is shock, it may be salutary; and, in any event, as we examine and praise *The Reeve's Tale*, we hope that we shall not seem to be suggesting that it is something other than a funny story.

THE REEVE'S TALE AND THE CANTERBURY TALES

The Canterbury Tales have come down to us only in a fragmentary form, presumably because when Chaucer died in 1400 he had neither completed the whole work nor even decided in what order the existing parts of it were to be arranged. Some of these parts are inconsistent one with another; for instance, in *The Manciple's Prologue* the Cook is reintroduced as being drunk and incapable of telling a tale, in a way that totally disregards his earlier introduction in *The Cook's Prologue* and the fragment of tale he then tells. If he had ever completed the work, Chaucer would doubtless have cancelled or modified one of these passages to remove the inconsistency. There is disagreement among scholars even as to the number of fragments into which the surviving parts fall and the order in which some of them should be read, but fortunately this disagreement does not affect *The Reeve's Tale*. This tale unquestionably belongs to the first fragment, which is itself one of the most fully integrated parts of the *Tales* as a whole.

The first fragment begins with *The General Prologue*, in which the 'Chaucer' who acts as our modest guide through the poem describes the company of pilgrims who set off for Canterbury one April morning, and explains how, under the direction of the host of the Tabard Inn (their starting-place on the south bank of the Thames opposite the tiny medieval city of London), they agree to engage in a tale-telling competition to pass their time during the slow journey to the shrine of St Thomas Becket. Each pilgrim is to tell two tales on the outward journey and a further two on the return, and the teller of the tale generally agreed to be best will be rewarded with a grand dinner at the Tabard at the expense of the others. Of this vast scheme, providing for some 120 tales, less than a quarter was ever completed.

At the end of *The General Prologue*, lots are drawn to decide who shall tell the first tale, and the lot falls upon the Knight. His noble story of love and war is set in ancient pagan times, and shows human beings as subject to the will of the classical gods in ways that both propose and question a serious philosophical interpretation of life. When it is over, the Host calls on a second respectable member of the party, the Monk, to tell a tale to equal it. We are led to expect a second story of the same kind; but, before the Monk can begin, a third pilgrim, the Miller, thrusts himself forward. He is, he announces, drunk, and he proposes to tell the next tale himself:

> For I wol telle a legende and a lyf
> Bothe of a carpenter and of his wyf,
> How that a clerk hath set the wrightes cappe.

At once the Reeve objects, on the moral ground that it is sinful to bring any man or wife into disrepute. We have been told in *The General Prologue* that the Reeve is 'a sclendre colerik man', elderly, thin and close-shaven, capable of inspiring fear in those with whom he has dealings, so his objection seems in character. We have also been given hints of something ecclesiastical in his appearance, for 'His top was dokked lyk a preest biforn' and 'Tukked he was as is a frere aboute', so his moral condemnation of the tale he expects the Miller to tell is subtly appropriate too. But one other piece of information in *The General Prologue* is relevant also: that the Reeve's original trade was that of carpenter. He may have this more self-interested reason for disapproving of a tale in which a *clerk* is to get the better of a *wright*. The possibility is allowed to remain in suspense while the Miller tells his tale – for his drunken boisterousness overrides all objections.

The Miller's Tale is set in Oxford, and concerns

Introduction

Nicholas, a student who has lodgings with John, a prosperous elderly carpenter with an attractive young wife, Alisoun. Nicholas attempts to seduce Alisoun, her resistance is a mere token, and they agree to take the earliest opportunity to go to bed together. Nicholas has a complicated plan to bring this about. He locks himself in his room, and waits till John gets worried about his non-appearance. John, a kind-hearted if silly man, gets so worried indeed that he eventually has the door of the room broken down. He finds Nicholas lying absolutely still, apparently in a trance, and does his best to rouse him. At last the student comes to, and tells John in absolute secrecy that he has discovered by means of astrology that there is going to be a second Flood, as great as Noah's, the following Monday. The carpenter is to hang three tubs in the roof of his house, supply them with provisions, and make a hole in the roof so that they can float away like boats when the water rises high enough. John, Alisoun and Nicholas are to wait, one in each tub; and John and Alisoun are not to exchange a single word, still less touch each other, so as to avoid sin.

John believes every word of this absurd story, and does as he is told. He is so tired with his exertions that when the time comes he falls quickly asleep in his tub. Nicholas and Alisoun then climb quietly out of their tubs, and are soon enjoying themselves in John's bed. But there is a further complication. Another young men has also felt Alisoun's attraction: Absolon, the fastidious and dandified parish clerk. He has tried all the ways he can to arouse her interest, but, since Nicholas is on the spot and he is not, he has had no

success. Having learned that John has not been seen
for a few days, he decides that this very night he will
knock at her bedroom window in the hope of gaining
a kiss from her. He does so, and Alisoun, more
agreeably occupied than she usually is at night, at first
derides him. But then she has an idea. Will he promise
to go away if she grants him a kiss, she asks? He swears
that he will; and she at once thrusts out of the window
not her mouth but her behind. Absolon kisses it, and
only then realizes what he has done, and is filled with
horror, quickly followed by a determination to take
vengeance.

Absolon goes quietly across the road to a smith, who
is working through the night on ploughing equipment,
and asks if he may borrow a red-hot coulter. The smith
is mystified as to what he can want it for, but agrees.
Absolon then returns to the window and begs for
another kiss, saying that he will give Alison a gold ring
if he gets it. Nicholas thinks that this time *he* will have
some fun, so it is his behind that is stuck out of the
window. Absolon applies the hot coulter, and Nicholas
screams for water. The noise wakens John, and when
he hears the cry of 'Water!' he thinks the Flood has
come, cuts the rope from which his tub is suspended,
and comes crashing to the ground, breaking his arm
as he does so. The neighbours gather to see what has
happened, and Alisoun and Nicholas persuade them
that it was John in his folly who imagined that a second
Floou was imminent and insisted that they should all
hang from the roof. The *clerkes* all stick together in
spreading this false story, and it is generally believed.

In a whole variety of ways, *The Miller's Tale*

provides a necessary context for the appreciation of *The Reeve's Tale*. Both tales are set in university towns (Oxford and Cambridge, the homes of the only two universities that existed in Chaucer's England). Both tell of mistaken identities and sexual misdoings occurring by night in the houses of prosperous tradesmen. In both, *clerk* is set against tradesman, and in both it is the *clerk* who gets the upper hand. This last similarity deserves to be expanded a little. In the Middle Ages, when literacy was far less widespread than it is now, the gulf between educated and uneducated people was very wide. At one time, literacy had been almost entirely confined to the clergy, and a *clerk* meant both a man in ecclesiastical orders (a cleric) and a learned man or scholar. By the fourteenth century, literacy was more common among the English laity, and there is no reason to suppose that successful craftsmen like John the carpenter or Simkin the miller were unable to read and write, at least in English, though they would have been most unlikely to know Latin, the language of medieval learning. There was still, however, a good deal of antagonism between the learned and the unlearned, as indeed there tends to be between town and gown in university cities today. In both tales, this antagonism is made explicit by the unlearned craftsman: with pious silliness by John –

> Ye, blessed be alwey a lewed man
> That noght but oonly his bileve kan!
> So ferde another clerk with astromie;
> He walked in the feeldes, for to prye
> Upon the sterres, what ther sholde bifalle,
> Til he was in a marle-pit yfalle;
> He saugh nat that...

– and with contemptuous irony by Simkin, when he suggests that the two students should use *argumentes* to increase the size of the cramped lodging that is all he can offer them. The conflict between *clerk* and layman, *lered* and *lewed*, is an important underlying theme in both tales. Both are ultimately told, as we shall see, from the point of view of the educated, to whom Chaucer and his audience belonged; though in tales where the *clerk* is not a lively young student but a monk or friar, the bourgeois laymen may get the better of him. Behind the antagonisms of individuals in Chaucer's comic tales we need to recognize the rivalries of various social castes and groups.

This brings us back to another way in which *The Reeve's Tale* springs from *The Miller's Tale*. As we have seen, *The Miller's Prologue* mentioned the fact that the Reeve had been a carpenter, but without drawing any conclusions from it. In *The Reeve's Prologue* Chaucer returns to this piece of information and makes its significance explicit, telling us that the only pilgrim who took offence at *The Miller's Tale* was Oswald the Reeve, 'By cause he was of carpenteris craft' (6). After Oswald's discourse on old age, dismissed by the Host as inappropriate *sermoning*, he reverts to this underlying grievance. He sees the Miller as having told of the deception of a carpenter, 'Peraventure in scorn, for I am oon' (61), and he announces his determination to get his own back by telling a story against a miller. In fact it seems unlikely that the Miller had Oswald in mind in telling his tale, and indeed John's craft as carpenter is of only minor importance in the story. It makes him parallel with Noah, who experienced the first Flood, and with Joseph, another elderly carpenter puzzled by his young wife's behaviour, and is expanded into various small details such as his ability to make ladders himself for the three to climb into their tubs, and his possession of an axe for cutting the rope. But Oswald, with a determined vindictiveness that cloaks itself in religious justification –

> He kan wel in myn eye seen a stalke,
> But in his owene he kan nat seen a balke   (65–6)

– directs his tale firmly against the Miller's craft, and the work and reputation of millers become a central element in his tale.

This ingenious linking of tales that might have been totally separate is continued in the final components of the first fragment, *The Cook's Prologue* and *Tale*. The Cook is beside himself with joy at *The Reeve's Tale*, and then offers to tell the next story himself. His tale is unfinished – indeed, is scarcely more than begun – so that we cannot know how fully it was to be connected to what went before, but two kinds of connection are suggested by *The Cook's Prologue*. The first is indicated by the phrase 'argument of herbergage' (475), used by the Cook to describe *The Reeve's Tale*. He is thinking back to Simkin's sarcastic proposal that by *argumentes* the clerks could make his narrow house more spacious, and he goes on to point out the danger – as Simkin found it, and John before him – of unwisely giving someone else lodging in your house. This is precisely what the master *vitaillier* has already discovered in the opening lines of *The Cook's Tale*, when he has Perkin living in his house as an apprentice. He learns his lesson in time, but perhaps it will have to be learned again by the crony to whose house Perkin then transfers himself. The second connection is brought out by the second half of *The Cook's Prologue*. There the Host, in agreeing that the Cook should be the next storyteller, chaffs him about the lack of hygiene in his shop; and this leads Hogge to threaten that his tale will be about an *hostileer* – someone of the Host's own profession – and that it may give him cause for anger. The following line – 'But nathelees I wol nat telle it yit' (507) – suggests, however, that the Cook is looking forward to some later story he will tell. Certainly there seems to have been a natural antagonism in Chaucer's time between those who sold food and those, like the Host, who provided lodgings but often added board as well. Once more professional and economic rivalries are to supply the motive power for the stories of individuals, and are thereby to place them in a more comprehensive social context. Whether the *hostileer* was to appear in the tale the Cook commences, and if so how he was eventually to be treated, we do not know, because Chaucer broke off after less than a hundred lines. What he wrote, however, is sufficient to suggest a third connecting link, in the broad contrast in theme between *The Reeve's Prologue* and *The Cook's Tale*. The former emphasizes the failings of age, the latter those of youth.

Despite its incompleteness, we have included *The Cook's Tale* and its prologue in this edition of *The Reeve's Tale*. We have done so for three reasons. One is already indicated by what we have written above.

Introduction

The Cook's Prologue and *Tale* are closely related to *The Reeve's Tale*, and their very brevity gives the reader an opportunity to study within a single volume Chaucer's methods of using the pilgrimage framework to connect one tale with another in a more than superficial way. The second is that *The Cook's Prologue* and *Tale* are in themselves admirable, though brief, examples of Chaucer's mature art: in their colloquial vigour of language and their shrewd selection of realistic detail, with its suggestion of a London scene observed with humour and relish, they are in no way inferior to the Miller's and Reeve's tales and their prologues. The suggestion which has been made that Chaucer broke off writing *The Cook's Tale* because he was dissatisfied or even disgusted with it, seems absurd, and could arise only from a dislike of the whole enterprise he undertook in his late comic tales. The third reason is that, by including *The Cook's Prologue* and *Tale* here, we are able to complete within this series of selected tales from Chaucer an edition of the whole of the first fragment of *The Canterbury Tales* – the part of Chaucer's final work that comes nearest to completion.

THE REEVE'S TALE AND THE FABLIAUX

Both *The Reeve's Tale* and the fragment of *The Cook's Tale* belong to a distinctive medieval literary genre, the 'fabliau'. This can be most simply defined as a comic short story in verse. It originated in French in the thirteenth century, and soon became popular in other languages too. Most fabliaux derive their comedy from sexual and excretory matters, and they frequently take respectable figures such as priests and rich bourgeois as the butts of their jokes. In English, unlike German or Italian, the fabliau is very rare as a written form in the Middle Ages, and this makes it all the more surprising that it should play such a large part in Chaucer's work. It seems to have been in the 1390s, the last decade of his life, that he began to write fabliaux. They are found only in *The Canterbury Tales*, where, besides *The Reeve's Tale* and *The Cook's Tale*, the tales of the Miller, the Friar, the Summoner, the Merchant and the Shipman all belong to this genre; thus *The Canterbury Tales* contains more fabliaux than poems of any other single literary kind.

Fabliaux are normally set in lower- or middle-class life, but this does not mean that they are in any important way the product of the lower levels of medieval society. They were largely set down for aristocratic and wealthy audiences. This is equally true of Chaucer's fabliaux, even though he clouds the issue in *The Canterbury Tales* by creating the fiction that the fabliaux are told by pilgrims from the lower and middle classes. In *The Miller's Prologue*, he describes the forthcoming story as a 'cherles tale', an example of *harlotrie* of the kind that must be expected from a *cherl* such as the Miller or the Reeve, and he uses this as his apology for sullying his listeners' ears with such deplorable filth. This too is part of the fiction, of course; Chaucer did not have to include such tales, or have such vulgar characters on his Canterbury pilgrimage, if he had not chosen to do so. His fabliaux are ultimately his own responsibility, and he wrote them for his usual upper-class audience. They are represented as being told by millers, carpenters or cooks, but they were certainly not written for millers, carpenters or cooks, and the attitudes they express towards the bourgeois life they represent, with its eager acquisitiveness and low cunning, are fundamentally the attitudes of aristocratic derision or contempt. Such fundamental attitudes may be subtly modified by understanding, relish, or even traces of sympathy, but they remain what they are, and they give to the fabliaux a bracing callousness, which some modern readers may even find too bracing.

The explanatory comment offered on Simkin's conception of the type of wife suitable to his own social position –

> For Simkin wolde no wyf, as he saide,
> But she were wel ynorissed and a maide,
> To saven his estaat of yomanrye   (93–5)

– though it purports to give Simkin's own view of the matter, in fact implies a viewpoint that is neither his nor that of the sour Reeve, but rather the easy and disengaged amusement of those to whom the calculation of social standing or difference at a level so far below them can only be ridiculous. Much of the distinctive comedy of Chaucer's fabliaux derives from the presentation of socially or morally gross subject-matter in a context which implies refinement and learning. Perhaps this context is less noticeable in *The Reeve's Tale* than in most of the other fabliaux of *The Canterbury Tales*, but it is present there too, for example in terms of French descent such as *ynorissed*, *mesuage*, *nicetee*, *suffise*, or *despitously*, and in the learned symbolism concealed within such solidly material things as mills and horses. We shall be returning to these topics later: here it is enough to say that for a full appreciation of Chaucer's fabliaux we need to recognize that they are doing two things at once: imagining the 'low' worlds they represent from within assumptions about reality that are attributed to those worlds themselves, and simultaneously placing them in a perspective derived from a 'high' (that is, educated and refined) point of view. The 'realism' of Chaucer's fabliaux, as we shall see later, can go remarkably far, but it is very different from the realism or naturalism of the nineteenth-century novel, of Zola or Gissing. That aims at a kind of neutrality in its presentation of the detail of real life; whereas the realism of the fabliaux is ultimately based on an aristocratic conception of lower-class life as comic.

One characteristic feature of the fabliaux – and this is surely the basis of their kind of realism – is their pervasive emphasis on man's existence as a physical being in a physical world. However ingeniously intellectual the calculations involved, the ends in view can always be defined in solidly material terms: the possession of another man's wife or daughter, or the gaining of a 'cake / Of half a busshel flour, ful wel ybake' (457–8). In sexual matters, the very specificity of what is aimed at keeps these tales in a quite different world from that of pornography, because they leave no room for private erotic fantasizing. In poems such as these, physical causes have inescapably physical effects: if you cut the rope when you are hanging from the roof in a tub, you fall down with a crash and break your arm; and if one line tells us that 'on the nose he smoot him with his fest', the other half of the couplet inevitably comes chiming in with 'Doun ran the blody streem upon his brest' (421–2). Men, women and children are urged by the undignified bodily necessities that they share with animals, and that somehow do not get mentioned in idealizing fictions such as *The Knight's Tale*. After an evening spent chasing their horse through the fen, Aleyn and John are 'Wery and weet, as beest is in the rein' (253), and have no choice but to swallow their pride and endure Simkin's heavy mockery, in order to gain lodging for the night and share his roast goose and 'strong ale atte beste' (293). And then, the consequence of an evening's drinking is slurred speech, heavy sleep, loud snoring, and later a need to relieve one's bladder. Again, the cradle has to be put at the foot of Simkin's bed, so that the baby's necessities can be served, and his wife can 'yeve the child to sowke' (303).

In this world governed by mechanical and biological necessities, the exact placing of objects and events within a restricted area of physical space and real time tends to be of crucial importance. The events of a courtly romance such as *The Knight's Tale* are spread out over many years and many countries (and behind them is a metaphysical space, occupied by gods, destiny, and an inscrutable 'First Mover', that seems of infinite depth). The events of *The Reeve's Tale* are compressed into at most twenty-four hours, comprising part of one day and the following night until some time after the third cockcrow. They are equally carefully located in a familiar space – a particular mill on the edge of the fen, 'At Trumpingtoun, nat fer fro Cantebrigge' (67). Admittedly the fen itself, especially as darkness falls, seems to take on a frightening depth that verges on symbolic possibility (passion? despair?); but the runaway horse is caught in a ditch after all, and the main events of the story are even more stringently compressed in the *streit* house of the miller, which no *argumentes* can enlarge, and where six people (if we count the baby) grope confusedly towards and away from each other in a single bedroom. Even the 'cake of half a busshel' is precisely located 'Right at the entree of the dore bihinde' (389); and the exact placing and re-placing of the cradle is of course essential to the plot. If the timing of the tale is to have its full effect, all such elements must be unobtrusively assembled and planted in advance; thus the child and its cradle are first mentioned at lines 117–18, long before they are needed, while Simkin's bald head, from which the moonlight will be reflected at line 447, is introduced at line 81, and perhaps alluded to in the 'by my croun' of line 245.

The moral space of Chaucer's fabliaux is less clearly charted than their physical space. Sometimes, characters may seem to receive punishments that are precisely adapted to their particular faults or follies. Thus in *The Miller's Tale* the ludicrously fastidious Absolon, obsessed with sweet tastes and scents, and forever spreading the smell of incense in church or sucking lozenges to make his breath sweet, ends by kissing Alisoun's behind 'ful savourly' and thereby is forever 'heeled of his maladie'. Similarly in *The Reeve's Tale*, not only does Simkin's pride in his ability to get the better of mere academics receive an unexpected fall, but his grotesque obsession with his own social grandeur and his wife's noble ancestry is at the same time appropriately punished when the students both *swyve* his wife and *disparage* the daughter whose virginity he has so carefully treasured. But things do not always fall out so aptly. In *The Miller's Tale*, John the carpenter, an amiable old man with a real concern for his lodger's health, does nothing to deserve his suffering, except by marrying a beautiful young wife; and Alisoun equally does nothing to deserve her total escape from the various punishments endured by the other characters, except by being young and attractive. And in *The Reeve's Tale*, while Simkin's wife might be thought to deserve to share his punishment, since she shares his pride, the same cannot be said of poor Malyne, his daughter. It is not her fault that her grandfather makes difficulties about her marriage or that her father takes such pride in her noble blood or his own skill as a thief. She has few physical attractions, and has been kept unmarried beyond the normal age for a girl of her time; her night with Aleyn is a far more significant emotional experience for her than it is for him, and she is almost weeping when she says farewell to him after an encounter that for her has been a moving romantic occasion but for him has been merely a means of *esement*. At the end of the story she is left unmarriageable, through the loss of her virginity, and with presumably little hope of seeing Aleyn again. But we are not invited to sympathize with her for more than the moment at which she sides with him against her father, and tells him where to find the half-bushel loaf. We are simply told, here and in Chaucer's fabliaux generally, to accept the fact that life is amoral, and that on the whole those who are young, attractive and cunning stand a better chance of success than those who are not. Perhaps that is what life is really like, though we might prefer it not to be.

The effect of *The Reeve's Tale*, with its callous and cheerful amorality, is something like that of a game.[1] The teams involved are town and gown, or *lewed* and *lered*. In the first half, the *lewed*, in the person of Simkin, have the best of the play. Simkin has taken the opportunity of the manciple's sickness to steal not just *curteisly* but *outrageously* from the Cambridge college, the King's Hall (143–4); the two students take up his implicit challenge on the college's behalf, swearing that

> The millere sholde not stele hem half a pekke
> Of corn by sleighte, ne by force hem reve.   (156–7)

Having arrived at the mill, they propose to stand, one by the hopper and the other by the trough, to make sure that nothing is stolen at either end of the milling process; but Simkin sees through their would-be cunning, and is only spurred on by it to greater heights of ingenuity:

> Al this nis doon but for a wile.
> They wene that no man may hem bigile,
> But by my thrift, yet shal I blere hir ye,
> For al the sleighte in hir philosophye.
> The moore queynte crekes that they make,
> The moore wol I stele whan I take.
> In stide of flour yet wol I yeve hem bren.
> 'The gretteste clerkes been noght wisest men'...
>   (193–200)

[1] See Glending Olson in *Modern Language Quarterly* XXXV (1974).

So he secretly looses the horse that the students have borrowed from the head of their college, and while they are desperately searching for it, he calmly steals half a bushel of their flour and tells his wife to bake it into a loaf, remarking with satisfaction, 'Yet kan a miilere make a clerkes berd' (242). When half-time comes, with the two sides sitting down together over a meal the students have promised to pay for (an event which occurs exactly halfway through the tale), it seems as though the game is already lost and won: the students, having listened to Simkin's crows of triumph over the impotence of their academic skills, are obliged to butter him up – 'Ay is thou myrie, and this is faire answerd' (274) - to persuade him to provide supper for them.

In fact, however, Simkin has already sown the seeds of his eventual defeat, by arranging things so that the two apparently beaten students have to spend the night in his own house. Aleyn is kept awake by the threefold snoring, and determines to get his own back, one goal for another:

> For, John, ther is a lawe that says thus,
> That gif a man in a point be agreved,
> That in another he sal be releved. (326–8)

He therefore creeps into Malyne's bed, and quickly gains satisfaction. John meanwhile burns with the spirit of emulation, and, by moving the cradle to the foot of his own bed, ingeniously arranges for Simkin's wife to join him. Thus 'This joly lyf han thise two clerkes lad' (378), and the score now seems to be Trumpington one, King's Hall two. But the game is still not over: when Aleyn leaves Malyne, intending to boast of his success to John, the shift in the position of the cradle misleads him, and he gets into bed with Simkin. When Simkin is told by him what has happened, he is naturally enraged, and a furious fight ensues. The outcome is determined not by cunning, but by pure chance – a force that in fabliaux tends to favour the young against the old and the *clerk* against the townsman. Simkin's wife, struggling to assist him, mistakes the glimmer of moonlight on his bald head – a marvellously incongruous poetic touch – for a nightcap worn by one of the students, and knocks him out with a stick. Aleyn and John callously beat him up as he lies unconscious, and ride home with their flour and the hidden loaf, having paid neither for the grinding nor even for their supper, and leaving his wife and daughter both *swyved*. The final score, then, is something like Trumpington two, King's Hall four; and the Reeve sees himself as having defeated the pilgrim-Miller by the same margin. We are left sharing his exhilaration, and with no concern whatever about the morality of the events he has recounted.

THE REEVE'S TALE AND ITS ANALOGUES

The elements which make up the plot of *The Reeve's Tale* are found in many medieval comic stories: the cradle-trick is particularly widespread. The same is true of *The Miller's Tale*, but there no exact analogues are known for the story as a whole, and we must either suppose that Chaucer put it together himself, or, more likely (for he was not in the habit of inventing his own plots), that he based it on a French fabliau which has not survived. With *The Reeve's Tale*, the situation is different. At least five medieval analogues are known, two French, two German, and one Italian (from Boccaccio's *Decameron*). They all contain the basic elements of the whole plot, and are all earlier than Chaucer's version. The closest of these five to Chaucer's work is a French fabliau, *Le meunier et les .II. clers* (The Miller and the Two Clerks). Only there is the clerks' host a miller by trade, only there does he attempt to rob his guests, and only there does the motif of the runaway horse occur. We cannot be certain that this specific text was Chaucer's source, but he must have been working with a version or versions pretty close to it. In one particular respect, though, Chaucer does not follow *Le meunier et les .II. clers*: he omits one plot-element, according to which the miller's daughter has to sleep locked in a bin, the key to which is then passed to her through a small opening; she is persuaded to let one of the students join her in it when he passes through the opening a ring he has taken from an andiron, which he says is made of gold and has the marvellous power of preserving its wearer's virginity whatever she does. It was perhaps equally important to Chaucer that this element was particularly unrealistic and that it was incongruous in terms of theme and character. In *The Reeve's Tale* he seems to have aimed at an especially full imaginative integration of the various elements of an existing story. As the editors of the most recent collection of analogues write, 'Chaucer is alone in making the seductions particularly ironical by emphasizing the snobbishness, fastidiousness, and social ambitions of the women, and the jealousy of the miller.'[1] Most of the aspects of this imaginative integration could be discussed through detailed comparison of Chaucer's work with *Le meunier et les .II. clers*. We do not, however, intend to adopt this method of approach, both because it would involved a disintegration of Chaucer's constructive achievement, and because we have no reason to suppose that he was writing for an audience with a full knowledge of other versions of his story and a scholarly wish to compare one with another.

THE REEVE AS TELLER OF HIS TALE

One change that Chaucer unquestionably made to his source was the attribution of the story to the Reeve, but the precise significance of this change is not easy to define. Nowhere in *The Canterbury Tales* does Chaucer aim at a total impersonation of a particular pilgrim in the telling of his tale. In a few cases, there seems to be no special link at all between a pilgrim and the tale he tells, though the rather precise appropriateness of stories to tellers in the first fragment may well suggest that, if Chaucer had ever completed the whole work, he would have ensured that there were always significant links between the pilgrims and their tales. In some cases, such as *The Merchant's Tale*, we seem frequently to hear the voice of the individual pilgrim giving his own slant to the story; but in *The Reeve's*

[1] Larry D. Benson and Theodore M. Andersson, eds. *The Literary Context of Chaucer's Fabliaux* (Indiana University Press, 1971), p. 84. This useful volume contains texts and translations of all the major analogues to Chaucer's fabliaux. It is in fact only Simkin's wife, not his daughter, who is snobbish, fastidious and ambitious.

Tale and most of the other fabliaux the normal voice heard is that of Chaucer himself, modified by various telling details which serve to suggest an individual narrator or one of a certain social class. This is not to say, however, that we can draw a sharp distinction between elements in the tale that in some way belong to its teller and elements that are totally irrelevant to him, or conversely between information about the teller that is significant for the tale and information that has nothing to do with it. The overall design of *The Canterbury Tales*, with the descriptions of the pilgrims' appearances and characters in *The General Prologue* and the numerous prologues and other link-passages that serve to characterize and dramatize them further, is such as to provoke any reader to think about a tale in the light of all that he can learn of its teller, and *vice versa*. Our own imaginations are spurred into activity: that was surely Chaucer's purpose, and there are rarely obvious points at which that activity must be called to a halt; though on the other hand, we ought not to confuse the creations of our own imaginations with certainties about what Chaucer intended us to think. Reading any of the *Canterbury Tales* in its dramatic context demands both imaginative responsiveness and common sense, and the fact must be faced that the boundary between those qualities will be drawn differently by different readers. We can therefore point out, with greater or lesser confidence, *possible* connections between the Reeve and his tale, but the final judgment of how much is implied by the juxtaposition of this teller with this tale will have to be left to the individual reader.

Introduction

Our first acquaintance with the Reeve comes in the passage from *The General Prologue* quoted on pp. 69–70. He is first mentioned a little before that, in a summary list of the final group of pilgrims to be described:

> Ther was also a Reve, and a Millere,
> A Somnour, and a Pardoner also,
> A Maunciple, and myself – ther were namo.

There he is placed in the same line as the Miller, but his description actually comes between those of the Manciple and the Summoner. On the Reeve's work and character, we cannot do better than to begin by quoting the relevant paragraph from the edition of *The General Prologue* in this series, by James Winny (p. 118):

The normal duties of a reeve were to superintend a landowner's estates and tenants. This particular Reeve seems to have combined some of the functions of steward and bailiff with his own proper duties: compare line 595 and lines 600–1. Chaucer's deeply perceptive character-study could be read simply as the description of a medieval type – the choleric man, physically lean and dry, crafty, ambitious and revengeful in temper, watchfully alert. But Chaucer's analysis of the Reeve takes him far beyond the limitations of medieval physiology. He sees, in the man's bony legs, his cropped hair and his habit of shaving 'as ny as ever he kan', the manifestation of a mean, uncharitable nature which makes the Reeve's subordinates go in dread of his malice. His aim in life is to get the better of everyone, and he ridicules the attempts of auditors to catch him out in the embezzling by which he has quietly enriched himself. By dwelling on the heath outside the town he shows his hatred of humanity, isolating himself like a wolf who rejects all companionship, and ingratiating himself only with those who have goods to steal. His chosen place at the back of the other pilgrims reveals a man too mistrustful of his fellow-men to expose himself. He expects of them the same contempt for human feelings, the same unscrupulous regard for private advantage, as dominate his own warped and spiteful existence.

To this we can add a number of points that seem to relate to the tale. We have already seen the relevance to the Reeve's response to *The Miller's Tale* of the fact that the Reeve was trained as a carpenter; and it is obvious enough that the sharpness, malice and determination to be dominant emphasized in the *General Prologue* portrait make it highly likely that the Reeve will see *The Miller's Tale* as an attack on himself and that he will respond as aggressively as he does. The fact that the Reeve comes from Bawdeswell in northern Norfolk (a place with which Chaucer may have had some connection through his acquaintance with its proprietor, Sir William de Beauchamp) will turn out to be unexpectedly significant for the tale. The two students come from the far north of England, and, as we shall see, Chaucer indicates that they speak in a distinctive northern dialect. The Anglian dialect of the Reeve's native place is only slightly represented in his speech, but it would have come somewhere between the students' Northumbrian speech and the more southerly speech of Chaucer's audience. The Reeve was therefore unusually well placed to understand the northern dialect and to represent some of its salient features to an audience of southerners. A final point of possible significance comes in the interest in horses obliquely indicated in the *General Prologue* description:

> This Reve sat upon a ful good stot,
> That was al pomely grey and highte Scot.   (617–18)

The Reeve is the only pilgrim whose horse is named, 'Scot' being a common East Anglian horse's name, and this, together with the emphasis on its excellent quality (by contrast, for example, with the rustiness of his sword), can reasonably be taken to indicate that he has a real interest in horses. This aspect of his character then emerges more fully both in his own prologue and in his tale. In *The Reeve's Prologue* he speaks of himself in 'horsy' terms, with reference first to his age and declining vigour – 'Gras time is doon, my fodder is now forage' (14) – and then to the youthful desires that he nevertheless retains – 'And yet ik have alwey a coltes tooth' (34). In the tale, the chief reference to horses comes in the section of the plot in which Simkin looses the borrowed palfrey, and the students have to spend much time and effort in recapturing it. This plot-element is found in *Le meunier et les .II. clers*, but there it is treated only perfunctorily, and we are never even told whether they get the horse back. In *The Reeve's Tale* it is developed far more fully, in a way which is realistic but which also has symbolic implications we shall discuss later. The whole series of horse references may have originated in this relatively trivial plot-element in Chaucer's source.[1]

The Reeve's Prologue, with its compressed yet admirably suggestive richness, offers an impressively intimate development of some of the implications of the more external portrait of *The General Prologue*. Here, as the Reeve speaks, he paints a self-portrait which may well be more revealing than he knows. *The General Prologue* does not tell us how old Oswald is, though it gives a general sense of elderliness, particularly in the long temporal perspective opened up by the

[1] Two minor references to horses in the *Tale* are found at lines 201 and 309.

remark that 'In youthe he hadde lerned a good myster' (615). That youth is now evidently long past. In *The Reeve's Prologue* Oswald not only tells the pilgrims explicitly, 'ik am oold' (13), but goes on, in his lengthy *sermoning* about the effects of old age, to depict himself as a man obsessed with his advancing years and with the consequent loss of youthful vigour, and especially of sexual potency. Indeed, there is an interesting contradiction between the self-righteousness of his initial denunciation of the *ribaudye* of *The Miller's Tale*, which he associates with youth, and the way that he proceeds to speak so longingly of youthful desires and eventually to tell a tale that contains almost as much *ribaudye* as the Miller's. Beneath his frighteningly dry self-mastery and self-sufficiency there evidently lie frustrations that he has by no means resolved into the serenity of age. It is true that in this 'confession' the Reeve is following a long tradition of medieval and late classical treatments of old age. The language may be his own, but the general conception of old age as a time of fear and misery rather than of serenity goes back, through a whole series of literary texts, to the Latin elegies written by Maximianus in the sixth century. But the derivative nature of the general idea is surely no reason for us to disregard Chaucer's rehandling of it so as to give a convincing effect of an individual speaking from his personal experience.[1]

---

[1] Contrast R. W. Frank, in *Directions in Literary Criticism*, ed. Stanley Weintraub and Philip Young (Pennsylvania State University Press, 1973), p. 55: 'repeatedly critics have characterized the Reeve and his Prologue as bitter. A "personal" quality is ascribed to the performance that seems unwarranted. The Reeve is simply

The ecclesiastical associations in the *General Prologue* portrait of the Reeve are also developed further in his own prologue. The way that his initial assertion of being past the follies of youth expands into a more general treatment of age and its vices is surely not just an example of a certain literary tradition, but reveals a deep-rooted tendency in his character to preach and moralize. We seem to hear a man who has listened carefully to many sermons, and perhaps preached a few himself to his neighbours, in his confident division of his material:

> Foure gleedes han we, which I shal devise –
> Avaunting, lying, anger, coveitise.   (29–30)

The Host certainly regards his disquisition as a *sermoning*, and prefers that men should stick to their own trades: 'The devel made a reve for to preche!' (49). The Host also asks, 'What shul we speke alday of hooly writ?' (48), and, though he is perhaps speaking rather loosely, equating any preaching with exposition of the Bible, there is in fact at least one scriptural reference in the Reeve's 'sermon', in the line 'We hoppen alwey whil the world wol pipe' (22) (see Luke 7.32). Chaucer's age saw the growth of the religious movement called Lollardy, under the influence of John Wyclif, and this, besides its heretical doctrines, was generally understood to involve a kind of puritanism, including personal reliance on scripture by layfolk and opposition to swearing and other kinds of *ribaudye*. Chaucer himself was associated with a number of the leading courtly sympathizers with this movement, and

talking as one cast in the role of the "old man" should talk. His performance is not an autobiography; it is a rhetorical device.'

30

it is at least possible that the Reeve is intended as a mild caricature of a lower-class Lollard. Whether or not this is so, Oswald ends his prologue with another, considerably more pretentious scriptural allusion. His anger against the Miller, hitherto repressed, breaks out viciously, and then he hastily covers it with a sanctimonious reference to a familiar saying from the Sermon on the Mount:

> I pray to God his nekke mote to-breke!
> He kan wel in myn eye seen a stalke,
> But in his owene he kan nat seen a balke. (64–6)

The vices that Oswald has recently been attributing to old men thus become reduced to a mere mote, while the Miller's imagined malice towards himself assumes the dimensions of a beam.

These various factors seem to us to add up to a convincing picture of a moralizing lower-class puritan, bitterly aware of the damage done to him by time, and much given to self-righteous anger against others, but quite unaware of his own moral faults, or of the application to himself of the very text he ends by quoting. The question remains, however, of how far this portrait of the teller should be seen as reflected in the tale. This is a matter about which critics have disagreed. One, for example, sees the whole tale as coloured by its teller's malice and self-ignorance: it is a comedy, certainly, but a 'comedy of utter moral self-deception', in which Oswald quite as much as Simkin is assessed by the harsh measure that he deals out to others. Thus the effect of *The Reeve's Prologue* is to point to 'serious moral implications' in an apparently trivial tale. Another critic argues that the

Prologue is scarcely at all relevant to the *Tale*: in the latter, 'The atmosphere of contest is rather at odds with the Reeve's supposed vindictiveness... There is nothing in the tale which develops the morbid concern with aging that dominates the Reeve's prologue or that even points to an old man as its teller.'[1] As we have suggested above, the matter is one on which Chaucer might have expected readers to differ. On the one hand, though the Reeve's own vindictiveness is found in the relations between miller and students in the tale, it has surely been transmuted into something lighter and less sinister; and it is difficult to see any realistic intention behind the attribution of such an energetically funny story to an aged puritan. On the other hand, *The Reeve's Prologue* hints at a sufficiently harsh discord within the Reeve himself, driven by conflicting impulses which he does not fully understand, for us to find an appropriateness in the very incongruity of the story he tells. Chaucer may compose his works in virtually self-contained sections, but the juxtapositions of those sections are hardly likely to be random. We may, according to disposition or mood, find darker notes of choler and moral judgement in the farcical tale, but without ever being able to be sure that that was what Chaucer intended. He sets our imaginations at work, and then leaves them to operate freely.

[1] Paul A. Olson, in *Studies in Philology* LIX (1962), and Glending Olson in *Modern Language Quarterly* XXXV (1974).

Introduction

An important book about *The General Prologue* describes it provocatively as 'a poem about work',[1] and shows in convincing detail how, in the descriptions of the pilgrims, their personalities and views of the world are intimately affected by their working lives. It is striking, too, how prominent daily work is as a theme of some of the actual tales. (Not all of them, for in courtly stories such as *The Knight's Tale* or religious ones such as *The Clerk's Tale*, work as a conditioning factor of people's lives is hardly present at all: there the ultimate realities are seen as emotional or spiritual.) But in the fabliaux, as we have seen, ultimate reality is material, and in the material world people have to work for their living, and their lives are shaped by work and the economic relations associated with it. It is therefore in the comic tales, told about and usually by characters who follow recognized crafts or professions, that the world of daily work is seen as the very medium of normal human existence. There is far more detailed representation of daily work in Chaucer's comic tales than in most of their sources and analogues; and the way it is represented reflects Chaucer's own double existence as courtier and civil servant. The viewpoint (as we have suggested earlier) is ultimately aristocratic and detached; but the eye is the sharply observant organ of a man who, after his early experiences abroad as a diplomat, held such posts at home as Controller of Customs and

[1] Jill Mann, *Chaucer and Medieval Estates Satire* (Cambridge University Press, 1973), p. 202.

Clerks of the King's Works. In posts like those he must have had much practical dealing with men of many different trades and professions, and must have gained a sharpened sense of the way economic pressures persistently mould most people's lives.

The Reeve himself is of course a working man, who earns a comfortable living by uncomfortable means. His delightful country house, 'With grene trees yshadwed' (*General Prologue* 609), is seen as belonging to no detached and static idyll, but as the hard-won product of a life spent managing land, livestock and other men, and keeping a sharp eye on accounts. In his prologue, the language in which he speaks of the ageing process is pervaded with recollections of the working life in which Chaucer himself was brought up. Chaucer's father and grandfather were successful wine-merchants, and it must have been from this background that he drew the elaborate image of man's life as a full cask of wine, the contents of which first gush vigorously out through the *tappe*, and then gradually decline to a mere trickle that splashes on the rim.

In *The Reeve's Tale*, the kind of work that is most prominent is naturally milling. Simkin and his family live surrounded by their work: their very lives are shaped by it and the economic relations into which it brings them with the outside world, and the whole tale is full of *whete and malt*, of *mele and corn*, of hoppers and troughs, of flour and sacks and loaves, and of images drawn from the same area – tares (146, 202), draff-sacks (352), and 'the flour of il ending' (320). We shall look more closely at the miller's work shortly, but first it is worth mentioning that the life of the clerks too is seen as bound up with work and money. The 'greet collegge' (135) can be identified with virtual certainty as the King's Hall, and such a college was, then as now, an economic unit as well as an academic institution. The academic background is suggested by details such as the miller's sarcastic references to *philosophye* (196) and *argumentes* (269), and by the students' quotation of legal maxims; there is however no indication that these Cambridge *clerkes* have any of the selfless devotion to books and learning of the 'Clerk of Oxenford' among the pilgrims. The material aspects of university life are more strongly emphasized, in the very fact, for instance, that Aleyn and John are brought into contact with Simkin through the need of their college to go outside Cambridge itself to get its flour prepared for bread and its malt for ale. (As Bennett points out, the slow Cam did not provide power for sufficient mills within the town.) Then there are further details such as the different responsibilities of the warden and manciple of the college. The King's Hall, quite as much as the mill at Trumpington, is shown to be part of the working world, the everyday or, as we sometimes say, 'workaday' world, the world, as the carpenter in *The Miller's Tale* puts it, of 'men that swink'.

Further aspects of this world are centrally placed in *The Cook's Prologue* and *Tale*. In the *Prologue*, we learn from the Host of the unsavoury but convincing details of the Cook's way of earning his living: pies reheated more than once, flies among the parsley, and the consequent food-poisoning. These are no fictions:

Hogge himself agrees that they are truths. And in the fragment of his *Tale* we are thrust into another side of medieval working life: the joys and miseries of apprenticeship, the normal means by which a boy could learn the specialized work that would eventually earn him a living. The fourteenth century was in general a period of conflict between masters (who were organized into gilds) and apprentices (who were protected by no such organization). London apprentices and workmen were among the sympathizers with the Peasants' Revolt of 1381. In *The Cook's Tale*, so far as can be told from the part completed, the viewpoint adopted is that of the masters, and, from this viewpoint, the joys seem all to be on the side of the apprentice, the miseries on that of his master. Perkin, apprenticed to a master victualler, apparently does no actual work at all, but spends his time and his master's money in dancing, gambling, and rioting about the streets. The master feels the effect of this where it hurts – in his accounts – and the apprentice-ship is brought to a premature end. A final glimpse of yet another way of earning a living is given in the lines with which the fragment breaks off: Perkin takes lodgings instead, not with a respectable hard-working master-craftsman, but with

> a compeer of his owene sort,
> That lovede dys, and revel, and disport,
> And hadde a wyf that heeld for contenance
> A shoppe, and swyved for hir sustenance.   (565–8)

The oldest profession is here put on a level with its many successors, as a type of work undertaken for *sustenance*.

Introduction

Chaucer's England was in most respects a pre-industrial society, in which by far the greatest proportion of the population was engaged in the unspecialized agricultural labour necessary for producing food. Though this activity is very commonly implied as a background to life in Chaucer's poetry, he never represents it directly: the only agricultural worker among the Canterbury pilgrims is the Plowman, and ploughing was sufficiently specialized work to take its practitioners well out of the common mass of agricultural labourers. Among the more specialized crafts, milling was one of the most prominent. The landscape of medieval Europe was dotted with more water-mills than churches; and, whether the mill operated by water (as in *The Reeve's Tale*) or by wind, it was particularly striking as an early example of the harnessing of non-human energy to serve human purposes. The purposes had to be served: bread, the staple food in western Europe, could not be made unless grain was first ground into flour; and ale, the staple drink, could not be made without malt, for which barley had to be ground. Previously, the work had been done by hand, separately in every household; and the invention of the water-mill, which seems to have reached Britain about the ninth century, permitted a great saving of labour. But the machinery needed for water-milling was expensive, and the cost of the investment could not be repaid, still less could a profit be made, unless it could be ensured that all the grinding in a particular locality was done for payment in cash or kind at the local mill. In the Middle Ages, the normal arrangement was that the lord of a district obliged all his tenants to bring their corn to be ground at the mill he erected for the purpose, and from which he took the profits. The term *sokene* (133) refers to this monopoly right to grind and receive payment, usually at the rate of one-sixteenth of the value of the grain. The miller would normally be the lord's servant, and would receive wages for his work. By Chaucer's time, it was possible that a miller might have bought the freedom of the mill from his lord, and be using the monopoly for his own advantage; it is not clear from *The Reeve's Tale* whether Simkin is in this position. But in either case, it was the miller who represented to the users of the mill a monopoly power that might be used arbitrarily or dishonestly. The popular reputation of the medieval miller was unfavourable.

The characterization of Simkin in *The Reeve's Tale* is fundamentally derived from the reality and reputation of his trade. He is a powerful man – *perilous*, as John warns Aleyn (335), and a good wrestler (74). Millers had to be, if they were to heave sacks of grain and flour about. He is arrogant and aggressive – a natural consequence of his muscular strength and his powerful economic position. He aspires above his proper social station – a natural consequence of his opportunities for becoming wealthy, and a common topic of satire against millers. Above all, he is a thief, 'And that a sly, and usaunt for to stele' (86). The accusation was often made against medieval millers, largely no doubt because the opportunities for theft were so great. Without staying to watch both hopper and trough, as Aleyn and John attempt to do, a customer could never be sure that all the corn he had brought to be ground was in fact being returned to him as flour. Even if a miller were really honest, he would doubtless be tarred with the same brush; with Simkin this possibility does not arise, since he takes a positive pride in his abilities as a thief.

In *The Reeve's Tale* then, milling provides a richly detailed material setting for the story and is also seen as giving the miller a specific place in the medieval economy and as shaping his character accordingly. The tale's realism is grounded in the most powerful controlling factors of human life – class, money, and, above all, work. But milling is also important in a different way, as supplying an important symbolic setting for the story, which makes a major contribution to its meaning. The unusually consistent realism of *The Reeve's Tale* is by no means incompatible with an unusually ingenious symbolism. The symbolism of the mill is of two kinds, sexual and religious. Milling, and particularly grinding, has long been a popular metaphor for sexual intercourse.[1] There is a long tradition of anecdotes and songs concerning millers in which the metaphor is elaborated in great detail, including, for instance, the dialogue between a wind-miller and a water-miller in John Heywood's *Play of the Wether* (printed in 1533), and more recent examples such as the folk-song *The Miller and his Lass*

[1] For what follows, see Beryl Rowland, *Blind Beasts* (Kent State University Press, 1971), pp. 125–6, and Ian Lancashire in *Chaucer Review* VI (1971–2).

collected by Cecil Sharp in 1906.[1] There is no such detailed elaboration in *The Reeve's Tale*, but the constant action of the mill provides an amusingly suggestive background to the sexual activity that takes place in the miller's house. Simkin is paid out for his dishonesty as a miller by the *swyving* of his wife and daughter, and thus the 'grindinge of the whete' (460) that he loses is not only the literal wheat but also the *swyving* itself. The metaphor is reinforced by Chaucer's use of a popular pun on the word *flour*. The 'flower' of something is the best of it, and so flour is the 'flower' of the wheat, as distinguished from the husks and bran. Similarly, the best part of a maiden is her virginity; thus the Wife of Bath, in one of many images in her prologue drawn from milling and its products, laments that in her own case, after five husbands,

> The flour is goon, ther is namoore to telle;
> The bren, as I best kan, now moste I selle;

and Chaucer's friend John Gower writes of Theseus' seduction of Ariadne that 'The ferste flour he tok aweie' (*Confessio Amantis* v 5382). In *The Reeve's Tale*, Simkin attempts to steal the flour that belongs to the students' college; in return, one of them steals the 'ferste flour' of his only daughter. When Aleyn, the hero of this exploit, vows revenge as he lies kept awake by the snoring of Simkin and his family, he threatens, 'Ye, they sal have the flour of il ending' (320), and that line puns on all three meanings of the word *flour* at the same time.

[1] See *Tudor Interludes*, ed. Peter Happé (Penguin, 1972), pp. 164–5, and *The Idiom of the People*, ed. James Reeves (Heinemann, 1958), p. 156.

The mill, then, is a place where rough justice is done through ironically appropriate repayments, and this structure of paying back or 'measure for measure' points to the significance of the religious symbolism of milling.[1] This indeed has not been traced back in written texts as far as Chaucer's time, but it seems likely that it is in the background of the tale. Simkin attempts to get the better of the *clerkes* by giving them false measure; he should have remembered the saying from the Sermon on the Mount which comes in the verse immediately before the one to which Oswald alludes in the final lines of his prologue: 'For, with what judgment you judge, you shall be judged; and with what measure you mete, it shall be measured unto you again' (Matthew 7.2). He is himself measured unto with the cheating measure he has used to others. God's judgment itself has been seen as a mill. The poet George Herbert wrote in the seventeenth century, 'God's mill grinds slow, but sure'; and in more familiar words, Longfellow wrote in the nineteenth century, 'Though the mills of God grind slowly, yet they grind exceeding small.' It would be misleading, doubtless, to see divine justice seriously at work in the mill at Trumpington, but it seems probable that Chaucer had in mind a kind of parody of God's grinding in the pattern of events there. That sort of parody of intellectual and religious themes is indeed typical of Chaucer's fabliaux.

[1] See Paul A. Olson in *Studies in Philology* LIX (1962).

THE HORSE IN THE REEVE'S TALE

What we have written about the symbolic implications of mills and grinding is not meant to suggest that *The Reeve's Tale* is an allegory, in which the real meaning is of an abstract or general kind, and that once it has been grasped the concrete substance of the tale can be forgotten. To read the tale in that way would be to impoverish it deplorably. A better analogy might be found in the use of symbolism in some of the pictorial art of the later Middle Ages, especially in northern France and the Netherlands. Here it frequently happens that a picture represents a scene with virtually complete verisimilitude, with all the details lifelike and sharply realized in themselves, and also fully consistent as a whole, but at the same time some of those details have further, symbolic meanings. This 'principle of disguising symbols under the cloak of real things' (as the art-historian Erwin Panofsky called it) is found particularly often in religious pictures, where details such as candlesticks, pieces of fruit and carafes of water, which may seem only to form part of the realistic setting of an Annunciation, really have symbolic meanings of their own, relating to the religious significance of the event represented. A particularly apt example is found in a threefold altarpiece by the anonymous Netherlandish painter known as the 'Master of Flémalle'. The main subject is the Annunciation, but one of the side-wings shows St Joseph working in his carpenter's shop. Joseph was commonly shown in medieval pictures and plays as a somewhat comic elderly workman, treated in fabliau terms as a supposed cuckold (John the carpenter in *The Miller's Tale* is obviously developed out of this conception of Joseph); and this is the figure realistically represented by the Master of Flémalle. Joseph has made a mousetrap, and displayed it on his windowsill to attract possible purchasers. Details such as that seem to belong solely to the Master's comic realism in representing a workaday world; and yet it has been pointed out that the mousetrap is an allusion to the learned theological doctrine of the *muscipula diaboli*, the devil's mousetrap – the idea put forward by St Augustine that the marriage of the Virgin to Joseph and the Incarnation of Christ were devised by God in order to fool and trap the devil as mice are fooled by the bait in a trap.[1] So this provides a particularly appropriate side-wing to a picture of the Annunciation. In *The Reeve's Tale* the main subject is itself secular, but there is surely a similar technique at work there, by which objects and events that form part of a consistent realistic surface also have disguised meanings, whether secular or religious.

Milling is one element of this kind; a further element, we suggest, is the episode of the horse. We have noted that in *Le meunier et les .II. clers* this is treated in a perfunctory way, as a mere excuse for getting the students off the premises so that the miller can cheat them. Chaucer, however, works it up very thoroughly in realistic terms. The reason why Aleyn and John are able to use a horse at all, despite the fact that medieval

[1] See E. Panofsky, *Early Netherlandish Painting* (Harvard University Press, 1953), vol. I, pp. 141, 164. For the general principle of disguised symbolism, see chapter v.

university students were not allowed to possess them, is explained in passing at line 221: they had borrowed it from the head of their college, who may have been allowed one at the college's expense. This detail adds to the motive of concern for reputation which is of some importance throughout the tale: they fear that the warden and their *felawes* will call them fools if they return to Cambridge without either horse or flour (256–9). Then, when the horse is loosed, it is on to a fen, populated by highly realistic wild mares, which it naturally pursues with a highly realistic whinny. There *are* fens around Trumpington, they did have wild horses running freely on them in the fourteenth century, and the fen itself adds in a most convincing way to the discomfiture of the students as they rush after their lost beast and get 'wery and weet' (253). Eventually the horse is caught in a ditch, and the episode concludes with John grumbling away as he leads it back to the mill. It is all delightfully lifelike.

It is also symbolic.[1] From the time of Plato onwards, the horse has been used as a symbol of the passionate side of human nature, the side man shares with the animals. One attractive medieval example of this is an ivory mirror case, carved with a scene in which the centre is occupied by a pair of lovers evidently about to embark on an affair, while to one side can be seen the heads of a pair of horses, which are having to be lashed by a groom to keep them under control. The horses form a witty comment on the tensions underlying the elegantly romantic scene next to

[1] See John Block Friedman in *Chaucer Review* II (1967–8).

them.[1] As the horse is a symbol of passion, so the bridle with which man controls it becomes a symbol of temperance; when temperance is not exerted, we still speak of 'unbridled' passions or lusts. In *The Reeve's Tale*, when Simkin 'strepeth of the bridel' (209) of the clerks' horse, he is setting loose dangerous passions in more than one way. The horse itself rushes off with a whinny of sexual desire in pursuit of the wild mares: the word *wehee* (212), representing the whinny, was used metaphorically in other medieval poems to indicate human lust in pursuit of its goal. And at the same time, Simkin sets loose passions he cannot control in his own house. As he lies snorting 'as an hors' (309), his own mares – his wife and daughter – are successfully pursued by John and Aleyn, to whom they offer no more resistance than, presumably, the Trumpington mares do to the college horse. Here too, then, the horse scene offers a marginal gloss on the main action of the tale. This is not to say that it can be simply translated into an explicit interpretation of that action. For example, though the clerks share their horse's rampant sexual potency, the passions by which they are driven are not only sexual. Aleyn's determination to avenge their loss, and John's wish to emulate his comrade, are the motives that lead them into the women's beds. The effect of the implicit parallel between the horse episode and the main topic of the

[1] The mirror case is in the Victoria and Albert Museum, London. There is a photograph of it in D. W. Robertson, *A Preface to Chaucer* (Princeton University Press, 1963), plate 63. Similar symbolic horses appear in other medieval representations of lovers.

tale is not to draw a specific moral but to incite us to think and feel for ourselves.

THE CHARACTERS OF THE REEVE'S TALE

Simkin

We have suggested that Simkin's character is strongly influenced by his way of life as a miller, as this was popularly regarded in the Middle Ages, and as it was in socio-economic reality. But neither his character nor that of the other persons in the story is fully determined by these outside factors: each has an individuality which, considering how short the tale is, is surprisingly strong and interesting. Simkin himself is certainly derived from the popular stereotype of the miller as muscular, arrogant and dishonest, but in him the stereotype undergoes subtle modifications. His arrogance, for instance, undoubtedly derives from tradition, and it is evidenced in many ways in the description with which the tale opens. He bristles dangerously with weapons – a 'long panade' with the blade of a sword hanging from his belt, a 'joly poppere' in his pouch, and a 'Sheffeld thwitel' in his hose (75–9): surely a superfluity of weapons, indicating showiness as well as danger. He and his wife wear red clothes, a colour that was forbidden to people of their social class. His prickliness encompasses his wife as well: no man dares to flirt or even joke with her, or else he risks being slain with one of Simkin's many blades (103–6). As the following lines hint, there is something showy in this intense jealousy too: it is evidently more a matter of what he wants his wife to think he feels than of what he really feels; and the fact that eventually John goes far beyond flirting with her adds a particularly apt touch to the humiliation Simkin undergoes.

Moreover, the specific form his arrogance takes, that of pride in his own social status, his 'estaat of yomanrye' (95), and in that of his wife and daughter, goes beyond the stereotype into an especially ridiculous area. He does not just ape his social betters, but becomes a living parody of their aristocratic concern with birth and breeding. The 'noble kin' (88) from which his wife comes means, at this social level, not aristocratic ancestry, but illegitimate descent from the parson. It was not uncommon in Chaucer's time for parish priests, who were of course supposed to be celibate, to have illegitimate children, but this was scarcely something to be proud of. Nevertheless, not only Simkin but the priest too takes extreme pride in his daughter and granddaughter, and the preposterousness of this situation is brought out in the harshly ironic lines in which the Reeve praises the parson's intention to provide Malyne with a dowry large enough to marry her into

> som worthy blood of auncetrye:
> For hooly chirches good moot been despended
> On hooly chirches blood, that is descended.
> Therfore he wolde his hooly blood honoure,
> Though that he hooly chirche sholde devoure.
>
> (128–32)

The snarling contempt of the repetitions of *hooly*, *chirche*, and *blood* is unmistakeable, and it brings to an end this initial statement of the miller's pretensions and the falsity and corruption that underlie them.

This note is never struck again in the tale, and indeed Simkin's social pride is now allowed to recede into the background, as the story concentrates on a different aspect of his arrogance, his determination to get the better of his supposedly learned customers. The disappearance of the theme of social pride, after it has been so fully developed in the opening section, may seem at first like miscalculation or forgetfulness on Chaucer's part, but in fact it is part of his careful plotting of the tale. The train of powder has been laid and lit, and it continues to smoulder silently as the action proceeds, until finally the explosion comes with the word *disparage* in the climactic moment at which Aleyn unknowingly tells Simkin what has been happening while he has been asleep:

> Thow shalt be deed, by Goddes dignitee!
> Who dorste be so boold to disparage
> My doghter, that is come of swich linage?   (416–18)

To *disparage* is not just to dishonour someone, but to do so by marrying her to someone of a lower social class; and it is this fundamental snobbery of the miller that comes to the surface at the moment of truth. He cares less that his daughter has been seduced than that she has been seduced by a man whom he sees as being socially beneath her. (In fact there seems little to choose between a 'povre scoler' and the offspring of a miller and a priest's bastard daughter.) Now we see the point of the initial elaboration of the particular form Simkin's pride takes, and it leads us to feel that scarcely any punishment could be too bad for him. It is satisfyingly appropriate that the only outcome of his father-in-law's intense concern with *blood*, in the sense of ancestry, should be the 'blody streem' (422) from someone's nose in which Simkin and Aleyn 'walwe as doon two pigges in a poke' (424).

One other aspect of the traditional miller stereotype which is amusingly modified in Simkin is that of sexual prowess. In folk-songs such as *The Miller and his Lass* the miller is a man of great sexual potency. Simkin, as we have seen, is a man much given to sexual pride, but it is a striking fact – and one that we might, if we chose, see as part of the elderly Oswald's vengeance against the vigorous pilgrim-Miller – that the only 'grinding' of that kind that occurs in Simkin's mill is performed by the two young men. Indeed, we are specifically told that when John was in bed with Simkin's wife, 'So myrie a fit ne hadde she nat ful yoore' (376). Simkin is exhaustively exposed as being all outside; inwardly, he is well past his best.

Simkin's Wife

Simkin's wife is less fully individualized than he is. It is perhaps significant that she is the only major character in the tale who is not named, but she nevertheless plays very effectively the part laid down for her. In her social pride, she is a mere echo of her husband, snoring in unison with him, following after him on holy days, wearing the same bright colour, so that 'A ful faire sighte it was upon hem two' (97). A nice touch is the addition that she was all the prouder

'for she was somdeel smoterlich' (109): her awareness
of her illegitimate birth does not lessen her snobbery,
but rather adds to it. As the tale proceeds, she appears
to understand little of what is going on, and her
attempts to intervene have precisely the opposite effect
to what she intends. She evidently does not know that
it is Simkin who has set free the students' horse, and
when she comes rushing in with the bad news her
complacent exclamations have a pleasing effect of
dramatic irony:

> Unthank come on his hand that boond him so,
> And he that bettre sholde han knit the reine! (228–9)

She little knows that *unthank* will indeed come upon
the responsible person, her own husband. She clearly
does not know that it is John, not Simkin, with whom
she gets into bed after she has risen in the night, though
she is apparently surprised by her partner's vigour.
Her exclamations when she is woken by Simkin falling
backwards on to her express the superstitious piety
that Chaucer often attributes to the lower-class characters of his fabliaux, and she once more speaks truer
than she knows when she cries out, 'Awak, Simond!
the feend is on me falle' (434) – it is no other devil than
her husband. Finally, when she loyally attempts to aid
Simkin in his fight, having carefully crept 'neer and
neer' with her stick (450), she hits the wrong man, and
is the cause of her husband's final defeat.

Malyne

Simkin's daughter, Malyne, is unfortunate enough to
take after her father in appearance, having his stocky

build and *camus* nose. The description of her at lines
119–22 is remarkably brief and downright; it contrasts
strikingly, for example, with the elaborate description
of Alisoun in *The Miller's Tale*. Yet it includes enough
to make it clear that she is an absurd combination of
a sturdy peasant girl with a heroine of courtly romance:
the 'eyen greye as glas' are a conventional feature of
such a literary heroine, and so is the fair hair which is
presented, honestly enough, as the one redeeming
feature of her appearance. We need to bear these
elements in mind when we consider her reaction to
having Aleyn in her bed: her feelings are those of a lady
of romance, a Criseyde when dawn comes and Troilus
must leave her. Almost weeping, she offers Aleyn the
only token she can of her affection: she tells him where
to find the loaf baked from the students' flour. The
incongruity of the emotion to its ignoble occasion
hovers between pathos and comedy. Malyne is a victim
of the situation into which she has been born, a mere
passive vehicle of the ambition of her father and
grandfather, and an equally passive means by which
they are punished. Aleyn may have promised to be
her own *clerk*, 'wher so I go or ride' (384), but it is
reasonable to suppose that he will not ride back to
Trumpington in a hurry. Yet, as we have argued, this
tale does not encourage us to dwell sympathetically on
her situation as it might if it were a nineteenth-century
novel. Malyne is no fourteenth-century Tess of the
D'Urbervilles, any more than May in *The Merchant's
Tale* is a fourteenth-century Connie Chatterley. After
her approach to tears at line 394, she plays no further
part in the tale.

Introduction

Aleyn and John

Aleyn and John, the two students, make themselves known to us above all as an inseparable pair. They come from the same part of the country, the 'toun ...that highte Strother' (160), and are evidently friends from before their days at Cambridge. The verse itself constantly pairs them together: 'John highte that oon, and Aleyn highte that oother' (159), 'Forth goth Aleyn the clerk, and also John' (164), 'Comth sely John, and with him comth Aleyn' (254), 'To bedde goth Aleyn and also John' (306). They speak to each other with the casual insults that are common among young friends: 'Alayn, thou is a fonne!' says John on learning that the horse (which Aleyn has evidently tied up) has escaped (235); and 'Thou John, thou swinesheed, awak!' whispers Aleyn as he tells him of his exploit with Malyne (408). *Clerkes* they may be, but we have no reason to suspect them of absorption in intellectual matters; though Aleyn can quote legal maxims to serve his own interests, and his ironic description of Simkin's family's snoring as *complin* (317) reminds one of the medieval link between learning and the Church. They are simply lively young men, with normal instincts and a good deal of animal ingenuity. Though they function largely as a twin-like pair, we can perhaps detect certain differences of personality between them. Aleyn is bolder and more confident: it is he who is the first to offer a breezy greeting to Simkin when they arrive at the mill (168), he who first determines to take vengeance for the injury done them, while John would evidently be content to sleep (315ff.), and he who cannot wait till they are safely away from the mill before telling his pal what success he has had with Malyne (405ff.). John is more cautious, reminding his impetuous friend that the miller is a dangerous man to trifle with (334–7); but on the other hand he is perhaps somewhat brighter, since it is he who knows the way to the mill, which was some way off the Trumpington road (166), and, more important, he who thinks of the cradle trick, a cunninger way of achieving his end than the risky direct method adopted by Aleyn. We cannot be surprised that Aleyn is the one who eventually gets involved in a fight with Simkin, while John apparently escapes unbruised.

Chaucer's most striking means of characterizing the two students is their use of northern dialect, and this is a major innovation on his part – there appears to be no earlier English example of the use of dialect for such a purpose. The fourteenth century was a period in which English rather than Latin or French was beginning to be the normal literary language for the first time for several hundred years; hence it was also a period in which people were becoming increasingly conscious of the different dialectal varieties of English spoken in different parts of the country. Chaucer's own English, that of the London area, is that from which modern standard English has developed, and already in the fourteenth century some southerners thought of northern dialects as inferior and comic. Major literature was in fact being written in such dialects – the superb romance *Sir Gawain and the Green Knight* is only one example – but the northern speech of Aleyn and John is clearly seen as comic by

Chaucer. It is persistently undignified, and at times produces turns of phrase that to a southerner convey something different from the speaker's meaning – 'I hope he wil be deed' (175) or 'Step on thy feet!' (220). It is one of the things that make us believe in them as thoroughly ordinary young men, with nothing of the excessive cleverness of Nicholas, the standard-Chaucerian-speaking Oxford student of *The Miller's Tale*. Indeed, their comic ordinariness gives a sharper edge to Simkin's humiliation: if he cannot outwit this pair, he can have little reason for his sense of superiority.

Chaucer does not attempt to make Aleyn and John speak a complete and consistent northern dialect. He does not tell us exactly where they come from, only that it was 'Fer in the north, I kan nat telle where' (161); and, inasmuch as we remember that the tale is being told by the Reeve, we shall bear in mind that their northern speech is being transmitted, plausibly enough, by a man from northern Norfolk, an area geographically and dialectally halfway between London and the north of England. Chaucer aims simply to sprinkle their speech with some of the most striking features of northern English, as these would attract the attention of his largely southern public. Within these limits, however, the work of modern philologists has shown that his knowledge of the northern dialect was remarkably accurate, and the students' speech can be identified as belonging to the Northumberland area.[1]

---

[1] The best studies are by J. R. R. Tolkien in *Transactions of the Philological Society* (1934), and R. W. V. Elliott, *Chaucer's English* (André Deutsch, 1974).

The chief difference in sound that marks off their speech from standard Chaucerian English is the substitution of long *a* for long *o*, so that they say *banes* for *bones*, *bathe* for *bothe*, *ga* for *go*, and so on. Short *a* is also substituted for short *o* when followed by *-ng*, hence *lange* for *longe* and *wrang* for *wrong*. The most noticeable difference in grammar is that in the third person singular of the present indicative, where Chaucerian English has the ending *-(e)th*, the northern dialect has the *-(e)s* that is normal in modern English: hence *has* (172, 173) instead of *hath*, *gas* (183) instead of *goth*, *wagges* (185) instead of *waggeth*. Chaucer also scatters about various northern forms of the verb 'to be' – 'I is', 'thou is', 'we are' (for southern 'we been'), and so on. So far as vocabulary is concerned, he includes quite a number of northern forms of common words, such as *swilk* or *slik* for *swich* ('such'), *whilk* for *which*, *til* for *to*, *sal* for *shal*, and also a fine collection of words peculiar to the northern dialect. Among these are *wight* 'swift' (232), *lathe* 'barn' (234), *ilhail* 'bad luck' and *fonne* 'fool' (235). As this group suggests, Chaucer tends to put dialect words and forms rather thickly in certain areas, rather than spreading them evenly throughout the student's speech. They are particularly frequent when they start speaking, so that we shall class them from the beginning as comic Northerners, and will perhaps think their dialect more consistently represented than it really is.

The originality of Chaucer's achievement in his use of dialect in *The Reeve's Tale* is remarkable. Nowadays the comic Northerner (or Welshman or West-countryman, or whatever it may be) is a familiar figure in fiction or on television, but Chaucer really seems to have been the inventor of this device. It is one of the many things that make *The Reeve's Tale* one of his funniest poems, and at the same time it contributes to the unusually elaborate localization of the comic anecdote in a particular time and place. Trumpington, Bawdeswell and 'Strother' all have their parts to play in an engaging and convincing picture of late fourteenth-century English life.

POETIC STYLE

The style of medieval poetry generally is more loose-textured, less compressed and richly metaphorical, than that of much poetry of more recent periods. There are several reasons for this, two of the most important being that a high proportion of medieval poetry was narrative, so that its style must be appropriate for story-telling, and that it was frequently composed not to be read privately and silently, but to be read aloud to listeners, so that it must not be so closely woven that an audience could not take it in. These generalizations apply to most of Chaucer's work. *The Canterbury Tales* of course consists largely of narrative, and, whether or not it was actually read aloud (Chaucer seems to have had in mind an audience of both listeners and private readers), the fictional situation it creates is one in which tales are spoken aloud to the company of Canterbury pilgrims, and the styles of the tales are on the whole appropriate to this situation.

On the other hand, as Chaucer's skill as a poet matured in the final decade of his life, he was capable of writing passages of a local depth and complexity unmatched by any other English poet before Shakespeare. We may perhaps suppose that it was his own earlier work that had elicited in his audience the taste and skill to appreciate such densely textured writing. One such passage occurs in *The Reeve's Prologue*, which in this way stands in sharp contrast with *The Reeve's Tale* and *The Cook's Prologue* and *Tale*. The *Prologue* begins quietly enough, with the plain narrative of the pilgrims' reactions to *The Miller's Tale* (though there is a pleasing hint of irony in the repeated 'A litel. . . a lite', for Oswald's anger, mainly suppressed on the surface, will in fact turn out to be far more than a little). But once Oswald himself starts speaking, the verse develops an unusual concentration of figurative language: the blearing of someone's eye, grass or dry food for fodder, a mouldy heart, the elaboration over five lines of the medlar image, dancing while the world pipes, a nail stuck in the will, the hoary head and green tail of a leek, and fire in the ashes. All these images are drawn from familiar areas of experience, and especially from the country life that was still close even to city-dwellers in the fourteenth century; they would therefore probably be readily understood, but they succeed one another with such rapidity that each is almost telescoped into the next.

The image of fire in the ashes is itself elaborated formally over three lines, and then further metaphors follow. First comes the colt's tooth, then the richly detailed image of man's life as a wine-tun, full at his birth, then gradually emptying as death draws its tap.

There is an admirable concreteness of imagination in the further development, as the liquid of life, reduced to a mere trickle, is thought of as splashing on the barrel's rim, and the splashing noise is paralleled simultaneously with the tedious chattering of an old man's tongue, and, through the pun on the other meaning of tongue, with a bell's chiming – perhaps that of a funeral bell. It is clear that this concentrated metaphorical texture belongs not to the whole prologue but to the Reeve himself: it is resumed, at a somewhat lower level, in his final words, with the images of setting someone's hood (making a fool of him) and – borrowed from scripture – of the *stalke* and *balke*, or mote and beam. It is perhaps only by chance that so many of the images in this passage present pairs in opposition: grass/*forage*, hoary head/green tail, fire/ashes, death/life, mote/beam – though this feature is generally typical of proverbs and similar nuggets of popular wisdom. But another element that helps to bind together the series of disparate images is the way that many of them are of whiteness in one form or another – the old man's 'white top' leads in turn to the whiteness of mould, the 'head' of a leek, and of ashes. Even his 'coltes tooth' gives a flash of whiteness too.

The poetic density of such a passage calls attention to itself, while the accomplishment of Chaucer's style in the following narrative, though no less great, is less striking and more difficult to discuss. In Chaucer's earlier work, his greatest achievement in poetic style is perhaps the gradual naturalization into English of a courtly high style derived from Latin, French, and above all Italian models. The culmination of this process is reached about 1385 in *Troilus and Criseyde*, Chaucer's longest and in many ways most ambitious poem. Subsequently, in *The Canterbury Tales*, this achievement can be taken for granted: further examples of courtly romance are found in *The Knight's Tale* and *The Franklin's Tale*, but Chaucer breaks new ground in the fabliaux, where he develops a 'low' style to match the undignified subject-matter – a style more closely related to speech, and making fuller use of the resources of popular, colloquial English. The distinction between 'high' and 'low', though it is one made by medieval writers on literary theory, and associated by them and by Chaucer himself with the upper and lower classes of society, is certainly not absolute in Chaucer's work. There had always been elements of the informal and the conversational in his most dignified style, while on the other hand, as we suggested earlier, even in the fabliaux the idiom implies an ultimately courtly viewpoint. Still, in *The Reeve's Tale* Chaucer moves as far as anywhere towards a verse style that gains its greatest power from common speech. The imitation of the students' northern dialect is only the furthest extreme of a tendency operative everywhere in the tale.

We see this, for example, in the many brief similes that are borrowed from spoken English. A high proportion of them employ alliteration, the commonest English device for conveying emphasis and linking ideas memorably together; and a high proportion, too, compare human beings to animals, and thus help to create the tale's undignified picture of mankind. They include: proud as a peacock (72), bald as an ape (81), pert as a (mag)pie (96), 'digne as water in a dich' (110), swift as a roe (232), 'Wery and weet, as beest is in the rein' (253), 'jolyf' as a jay (300), 'as an hors he fnorteth in his sleep' (309), lie like a draff-sack (352), and wallow like pigs in a poke (424). *The Cook's Tale*, evidently planned to continue in the same style, has three similar comparisons: 'gaillard' as a goldfinch (513), brown as a berry (514), and as full as a hive of honey (519).

Another way in which the style of these two tales draws on the strength of the native language is in the use of proverbs and generalizations of a proverbial type – terse and often concrete summations of common experience. Here indeed we see how impossible it is to draw a sharp distinction between 'low' and 'high', or popular and learned, in Chaucer's style. Just as, in *The Reeve's Prologue*, images drawn from everyday life mingle with those drawn from Scripture, so everyday proverbs are used in the same way as legal maxims, to offer authoritative support for a particular course of action, or to show how what happens exemplifies some general truth. *Sententia*, or moral generalization, is a favourite device of medieval rhetoric, and it can be supplied from either popular or learned sources. It is hard to know whether to classify Oswald's maxim in his prologue – 'For leveful is with force force of-showve' (58) – as part of his legal learning or as an instance of folk-wisdom; and indeed in a reeve's real life these two areas could hardly have been kept separate.

Examples from *The Reeve's Tale* include the following. John assures Simkin, somewhat ruefully, that 'nede has na peer', and immediately proceeds to add another stoical proverb, 'Him boes serve himself that has na swain', which he attributes to *clerkes*, though there is no reason to suppose it to be of learned origin (172–4). Simkin in return silently quotes to himself another proverbial truth, this time borrowed from a beast-fable: 'The gretteste clerkes been noght wisest men' (200). Later John quotes another bit of northern wisdom, which like his previous proverb acknowledges that man can only bow before adversity and make the best of it:

> I have herd seid, 'man sal taa of twa thinges
> Slik as he findes, or taa slik as he bringes'.   (275–6)

In the same speech he quotes yet another pessimistic general truth: 'With empty hand men may na haukes tulle' (280). Aleyn's turn comes next, and his *sententia* is both more optimistic and apparently learned:

> For, John, ther is a lawe that says thus,
> That gif a man in a point be agreved,
> That in another he sal be releved.   (326–8)

John cheers himself up with a proverbial encouragement: '"Unhardy is unseely," thus men saith' (356). And the tale ends with a pair of proverbs, both extremely well known, the first more colloquial in its wording and the second more learned:

> And therfore this proverbe is seid ful sooth,
> 'Him thar nat wene wel that yvele dooth';
> A gilour shal himself bigiled be.   (465–7)

A number of these *sententiae* from *The Reeve's Tale* have a northern dialectal colouring and can appropriately be associated, in context, with the Bawdeswell Reeve or the students from Strother. People have always liked to think of pithy truths as emerging from the wisdom of provincial communities. But in fact there is, if anything, an even higher concentration of *sententiae* in *The Cook's Prologue* and *Tale*, with their London ambience. The Cook himself begins by quoting a scriptural proverb, which he wrongly attributes to Solomon: 'Ne bring nat every man into thyn hous' (477). Then he quotes a strikingly compressed saying which he attributes to the Flemings: '"sooth pley, quaad pley," as the Fleming seith' (503) – another example, perhaps of a general preference for some element of strangeness or difficulty in the wording of general truths. In the fragment of his tale, the Cook quotes one proverb (in disguise, but betrayed by the concreteness of *wrothe*) –

> Revel and trouthe, as in a lowe degree,
> They been ful wrothe al day, as men may see (543–4)

– and another that openly proclaims its nature and its country origins:

> a proverbe that seith this same word,
> 'Wel bet is roten appul out of hoord
> Than that it rotie al the remenaunt'.   (551–3)

It is not only comparisons and proverbs that give *The Reeve's Tale* and *The Cook's Tale* their colloquial force. *The Reeve's Tale* in particular contains a very large number of words belonging to a colloquial register which are found nowhere else in Chaucer. Many of these are northernisms, which naturally enough are heard on the lips of the only characters whom Chaucer makes speak in northern dialect; but there are also a great many words evidenced in other southern texts, but not in any of Chaucer's other works. Among these are *camus* (80, 120); *panade* (75); *poppere* (77); *thwitel* (79); *hoker* and *bisemare* (111); *sokene* (135); *chalons* (286); *yexeth* (297); *quakke* (298); *crowke* (304); *daf* and *cokenay* (354); *unhardy* (356); *toty* (399). There are also a good many strongly-flavoured colloquial phrases, such as 'make a clerkes berd' (242), 'vernisshed his heed' (295), 'So was hir joly whistle wel ywet' (301), 'the flour of il ending' (320), and 'I is but an ape' (348). The prevalence of terms and phrases such as these is perhaps the chief factor in creating the impression that in *The Reeve's Tale* we delve deeper into common speech and common life than anywhere else in Chaucer's work.

Finally, though, a word must be said about a less obtrusive but probably equally important aspect of Chaucer's colloquial English, and that is its syntax. Part of the achievement of Chaucer's courtly style was the development of a highly complex syntactical structure: long sentences, rhythmically and dramatically organized with many subordinate clauses, making much use of relative and absolute constructions, and often diverging widely from the word-order natural to English, to follow patterns derived from Latin and Italian. For the fabliaux, and especially those parts of them that consist of colloquial dialogue and rapid action – which account for a large proportion of any fabliau – Chaucer tends to move away from this achievement, though without ever abandoning it entirely. His sentences and their clauses become shorter, and co-ordination replaces subordination in linking statements, with simple conjunctions such as *for*, *but*, and above all *and*.

A good example of this style, to convey a series of rapidly successive actions building up to a violent climax, can be found towards the end of *The Reeve's Tale*. In the following passage, the conjunctions are italicized:

> This John stirte up as faste as evere he mighte,
> *And* graspeth by the walles to *and* fro,
> To finde a staf; *and* she stirte up also,
> *And* knew the estres bet than dide this John,
> *And* by the wal a staf she foond anon,
> *And* saugh a litel shimering of a light,
> *For* at an hole in shoon the moone bright;
> *And* by that light she saugh hem bothe two,
> *But* sikerly she niste who was who,
> *But as* she saugh a whit thing in hir ye,
> *And* whan she gan this white thing espie,
> She wende the clerk hadde wered a volupeer,
> *And* with the staf she drow ay neer *and* neer,
> *And* wende han hit this Aleyn at the fulle,
> *And* smoot the millere on the piled skulle,
> That doun he goth, *and* cride, 'Harrow! I die!'
>
> (438–53)

There are a few subordinate clauses here, but they are on such a small scale as to be scarcely noticeable. We can observe strikingly colloquial effects in places where it would be normal in written English to use a relative construction, but this is avoided by repetition, as in 'a whit thing...this white thing' (447–8). Again, in his courtly style, Chaucer would not have made line 451 a separate statement, but would have been more likely to write something like, 'Wening han hit...'. The fabliau style helps to create the impression of a world full of violent yet disorganized activity, and one where action is more important than explanation or understanding. To fit such a style so smoothly into verse, without dropping into monotony or clumsiness, is an achievement that depends on not calling attention to itself, and that may therefore not bring Chaucer due credit.

NOTE ON THE TEXT

The text which follows is based upon that of F. N. Robinson (*The Complete Works of Geoffrey Chaucer*, 2nd ed., 1957). The punctuation has been revised, with special reference to the exclamation marks. Spelling has been partly rationalized, by substituting *i* and *y* wherever the change does not affect the semantic value of the word. Thus *smylyng* becomes 'smiling', and *nyghtyngale* 'nightingale', but *wyn* (wine), *lyk* (like), and *fyr* (fire) are allowed to stand.

No accentuation has been provided in this text, for two reasons. First, because it produces a page displeasing to the eye; secondly, because it no longer seems necessary or entirely reliable in the light of modern scholarship. It is not now thought that the later works of Chaucer were written in a ten-syllable line from which no variation was permissible. The correct reading of a line of Chaucer is now seen to be more closely related to the correct reading of a comparable line of prose with phrasing suited to the rhythms of speech. This allows the reader to be more flexible in his interpretation of the line, and makes it unreasonably pedantic to provide a rigid system of accentuation.

NOTE ON PRONUNCIATION

These equivalences are intended to offer only a rough guide. For further detail, see the Introductory Volume to this series.

ă represents the sound now written *u*, as in 'cut'
ĕ as in modern 'set'
ĭ as in modern 'is'
ŏ as in modern 'top'
ŭ as in modern 'put' (not as in 'cut')
final -*e* represents the neutral vowel. sound in '*about*' or '*attention*'. It is silent when the next word in the line begins with a vowel or an *h*.

67

Note on the text

$\bar{a}$ as in modern 'car' (not as in 'name')

$\bar{e}$ (open—i.e. where the equivalent modern word is spelt with *ea*) as in modern 'there'

$\bar{e}$ (close—i.e. where the equivalent modern word is spelt with *ee* or *e*) represents the sound now written *a* as in 'take'

$\bar{\imath}$ as in modern 'machine' (not as in 'like')

$\bar{o}$ (open—i.e. where the equivalent modern vowel is pronounced as in 'br*o*ther', 'm*oo*d', or 'g*oo*d') represents the sound now written *aw* as in 'fawn'

$\bar{o}$ (close—i.e. where the equivalent modern vowel is pronounced as in 'r*oa*d') as in modern 'note'

$\bar{u}$ as in French *tu* or German *Tür*

DIPHTHONGS

ai and *ei* both roughly represent the sound now written *i* or *y* as in 'die' or 'dye'

au and *aw* both represent the sound now written *ow* or *ou* as in 'now' or 'pounce'

ou and *ow* have two pronunciations: as in *through* where the equivalent modern vowel is pronounced as in 'through' or 'mouse'; and as in *pounce* where the equivalent modern vowel is pronounced as in 'know' or 'thought'

WRITING OF VOWELS AND DIPHTHONGS

A long vowel is often indicated by doubling, as in *roote* or *eek*. The $\bar{u}$ sound is sometimes represented by an *o* as in *yong*. The *au* sound is sometimes represented by an *a*, especially before *m* or *n*, as in *cha(u)mbre* or *cha(u)nce*.

CONSONANTS

Largely as in modern English, except that many consonants now silent were still pronounced. *Gh* was pronounced as in Scottish 'lo*ch*', and both consonants should be pronounced in such groups as the following: '*gn*acchen', '*kn*ave', 'wo*rd*', 'fo*lk*', '*wr*ong'.

THE PORTRAITS OF THE REEVE
AND THE COOK

(from *The General Prologue*, lines 589–624 and
381–389)

The Reve was a sclendre colerik man.
His berd was shave as ny as ever he kan;
His heer was by his eris ful round yshorn;
His top was dokked lyk a preest biforn.
Ful longe were his legges and ful lene,
Ylik a staf, ther was no calf ysene.
Wel koude he kepe a gerner and a binne;
Ther was noon auditour koude on him winne.
Wel wiste he by the droghte and by the reyn
The yeldinge of his seed and of his greyn.
His lordes sheep, his neet, his dayerie,
His swyn, his hors, his stoor, and his pultrie
Was hoolly in this Reves governinge,
And by his covenant yaf the rekeninge,
Syn that his lord was twenty yeer of age.
Ther koude no man bringe him in arrerage.
Ther nas baillif, ne hierde, nor oother hine,
That he ne knew his sleighte and his covine;
They were adrad of him as of the deeth.
His woning was ful faire upon an heeth;
With grene trees yshadwed was his place.
He koude bettre than his lord purchace.
Ful riche he was astored prively:
His lord wel koude he plesen subtilly,
To yeve and lene him of his owene good,
And have a thank, and yet a cote and hood.
In youthe he hadde lerned a good myster;

69

The Portraits of the Reeve and the Cook

He was a wel good wrighte, a carpenter,
This Reve sat upon a ful good stot,
That was al pomely grey and highte Scot.
A long surcote of pers upon he hade,
And by his side he baar a rusty blade.
Of Northfolk was this Reve of which I telle,
Biside a toun men clepen Baldeswelle.
Tukked he was as is a frere aboute,
And evere he rood the hindreste of oure route.

A Cook they hadde with hem for the nones
To boille the chiknes with the marybones,
And poudre-marchant tart and galingale.
Wel koude he knowe a draughte of Londoun ale.
He koude rooste, and sethe, and broille, and frie,
Maken mortreux, and wel bake a pie.
But greet harm was it, as it thoughte me,
That on his shine a mormal hadde he.
For blankmanger, that made he with the beste.

THE REEVE'S PROLOGUE

The prologe of the Reves Tale

Whan folk hadde laughen at this nice cas
Of Absolon and hende Nicholas,
Diverse folk diversely they seide,
But for the moore part they loughe and pleyde.
Ne at this tale I saugh no man him greve,
But it were oonly Osewold the Reve
By cause he was of carpenteris craft,
A litel ire is in his herte ylaft;
He gan to grucche, and blamed it a lite.
  'So theek,' quod he, 'ful wel koude I thee   10
    quite
With blering of a proud milleres ye,
If that me liste speke of ribaudye.
But ik am oold, me list not pley for age;
Gras time is doon, my fodder is now forage;
This white top writeth mine olde yeris;
Myn herte is also mowled as mine heris,
But if I fare as dooth an open-ers—
That ilke fruit is ever lenger the wers,
Til it be roten in mullok or in stree.   20
We olde men, I drede, so fare we:
Til we be roten, kan we nat be ripe;
We hoppen alwey whil the world wol pipe.
For in oure wil ther stiketh evere a nail,
To have an hoor heed and a grene tail,
As hath a leek; for thogh oure might be goon,
Oure wil desireth folie evere in oon.
For whan we may nat doon, than wol we speke;

71

Yet in oure asshen olde is fyr yreke.

Foure gleedes han we, which I shal devise—
30 Avaunting, lying, anger, coveitise;
Thise foure sparkles longen unto eelde.
Oure olde lemes mowe wel been unweelde,
But wil ne shal nat faillen, that is sooth.
And yet ik have alwey a coltes tooth,
As many a yeer as it is passed henne
Sin that my tappe of lif bigan to renne.
For sikerly, whan I was bore, anon
Deeth drough the tappe of lyf and leet it gon;
And ever sithe hath so the tappe yronne
40 Til that almoost al empty is the tonne.
The streem of lyf now droppeth on the chimbe.
The sely tonge may wel ringe and chimbe
Of wrecchednesse that passed is ful yoore;
With olde folk, save dotage, is namoore.'

Whan that oure Hoost hadde herd this sermoning
He gan to speke as lordly as a king.
He seide, 'What amounteth al this wit?
What shul we speke alday of hooly writ?
The devel made a reve for to preche,
50 Or of a soutere a shipman or a leche.
Sey forth thy tale, and tarie nat the time.
Lo Depeford! and it is half-wey prime.
Lo Grenewich, ther many a shrewe is inne!
It were al time thy tale to biginne.'

'Now, sires,' quod this Osewold the Reve,
'I pray yow alle that ye nat yow greve,
Thogh I answere, and somdeel sette his howve;
For leveful is with force force of-showve.

This dronke Millere hath ytoold us heer

72

How that bigiled was a carpenteer,   60
Peraventure in scorn, for I am oon.
And, by youre leve, I shal him quite anoon;
Right in his cherles termes wol I speke.
I pray to God his nekke mote to-breke!
He kan wel in myn eye seen a stalke,
But in his owene he kan nat seen a balke.'

THE REEVE'S TALE

Heere biginneth the Reves Tale.

At Trumpingtoun, nat fer fro Cantebrigge,
Ther gooth a brook, and over that a brigge,
Upon the whiche brook ther stant a melle;
And this is verray sooth that I yow telle:
A millere was ther dwellinge many a day.
As any pecok he was proud and gay.
Pipen he koude and fisshe, and nettes beete,
And turne coppes, and wel wrastle and sheete;
Ay by his belt he baar a long panade,
And of a swerd ful trenchant was the blade.
A joly poppere baar he in his pouche;
Ther was no man, for peril, dorste him touche.
A Sheffeld thwitel baar he in his hose.
Round was his face, and camus was his nose;
As piled as an ape was his skulle.
He was a market-betere atte fulle.
Ther dorste no wight hand upon him legge,
That he ne swoor he sholde anon abegge.
A theef he was for sothe of corn and mele,
And that a sly, and usaunt for to stele.
His name was hoote deynous Simkin.
A wyf he hadde, ycomen of noble kin;
The person of the toun hir fader was.
With hire he yaf ful many a panne of bras,
For that Simkin sholde in his blood allye.
She was yfostred in a nonnerye;
For Simkin wolde no wyf, as he saide,

74

But she were wel ynorissed and a maide,
To saven his estaat of yomanrye.
And she was proud, and peert as is a pye.
A ful fair sighte was it upon hem two;
On halydayes biforn hire wolde he go
With his tipet bounden aboute his heed,
And she cam after in a gyte of reed;
And Simkin hadde hosen of the same.
Ther dorste no wight clepen hire but 'dame';
Was noon so hardy that wente by the weye
That with hire dorste rage or ones pleye,
But if he wolde be slain of Simkin
With panade, or with knyf, or boidekin.
For jalous folk ben perilous everemo—
Algate they wolde hire wives wenden so,
And eek, for she was somdel smoterlich,
She was as digne as water in a dich,
And ful of hoker and of bisemare.
Hir thoughte that a lady sholde hire spare,
What for hire kinrede and hir nortelrie
That she hadde lerned in the nonnerie.

   A doghter hadde they bitwixe hem two
Of twenty yeer, withouten any mo,
Savinge a child that was of half yeer age;
In cradel it lay and was a propre page.
This wenche thikke and wel ygrowen was,
With kamus nose, and eyen greye as glas,
With buttokes brode, and brestes rounde and hye;
But right fair was hire heer, I wol nat lie.
   This person of the toun, for she was feir,
In purpos was to maken hire his heir,
Bothe of his catel and his mesuage,

And straunge he made it of hir mariage.
His purpos was for to bistowe hire hye
Into som worthy blood of auncetrye;
For hooly chirches good moot been despended
On hooly chirches blood, that is descended.
Therfore he wolde his hooly blood honoure,
Though that he hooly chirche sholde devoure.

Greet sokene hath this millere, out of doute,
With whete and malt of al the land aboute;
And nameliche ther was a greet collegge
Men clepen the Soler Halle at Cantebregge;
Ther was hir whete and eek hir malt ygrounde.
And on a day it happed, in a stounde,
Sik lay the maunciple on a maladye;
Men wenden wisly that he sholde die.
For which this millere stal bothe mele and corn
An hundred time moore than biforn;
For therbiforn he stal but curteisly,
But now he was a theef outrageously,
For which the wardeyn chidde and made fare.
But therof sette the millere nat a tare;
He craketh boost, and swoor it was nat so.

Thanne were ther yonge povre scholers two,
That dwelten in this halle, of which I seye.
Testif they were, and lusty for to pleye,
And, oonly for hire mirthe and revelrye,
Upon the wardeyn bisily they crye,
To yeve hem leve, but a litel stounde,
To goon to mille and seen hir corn ygrounde;
And hardily they dorste leye hir nekke
The millere sholde not stele hem half a pekke
Of corn by sleighte, ne by force hem reve;

130

140

150

76

And at the laste the wardeyn yaf hem leve.
John highte that oon, and Aleyn highte that oother;
Of o toun were they born, that highte Strother,   160
Fer in the north, I kan nat telle where.

  This Aleyn maketh redy al his gere,
And on an hors the sak he caste anon.
Forth goth Aleyn the clerk, and also John,
With good swerd and with bokeler by hir side.
John knew the wey, – hem nedede no gyde, –
And at the mille the sak adoun he layth.
Aleyn spak first, 'Al hail, Simond, y-faith!
Hou fares thy faire doghter and thy wyf?'

  'Aleyn, welcome,' quod Simkin, 'by my lyf!   170
And John also, how now, what do ye heer?'

  'Simond,' quod John, 'by God, nede has na
    peer.
Him boes serve himself that has na swain,
Or elles he is a fool, as clerkes sayn.
Oure manciple, I hope he wil be deed,
Swa werkes ay the wanges in his heed;
And forthy is I come, and eek Alayn,
To grinde oure corn and carie it ham again;
I pray yow spede us heythen that ye may.'

  'It shal be doon,' quod Simkin, 'by my fay!   180
What wol ye doon whil that it is in hande?'

  'By God, right by the hopur wil I stande,'
Quod John, 'and se howgates the corn gas in.
Yet saugh I nevere, by my fader kin,
How that the hopur wagges til and fra.'

  Aleyn answerde, 'John, and wiltow swa?
Thanne wil I be binethe, by my croun,
And se how that the mele falles doun

Into the trough; that sal be my disport.
190 For John, y-faith, I may been of youre sort;
I is as ille a millere as ar ye.'
   This millere smiled of hir nicetee,
And thoghte, 'Al this nis doon but for a wile.
They wene that no man may hem bigile,
But by my thrift, yet shal I blere hir ye,
For al the sleighte in hir philosophye.
The moore queynte crekes that they make,
The moore wol I stele whan I take.
In stide of flour yet wol I yeve hem bren.
200 "The gretteste clerkes been noght wisest men,"
As whilom to the wolf thus spak the mare.
Of al hir art ne counte I noght a tare.'
   Out at the dore he gooth ful prively,
Whan that he saugh his time, softely.
He looketh up and doun til he hath founde
The clerkes hors, ther as it stood ybounde
Bihinde the mille, under a levesel;
And to the hors he goth him faire and wel;
He strepeth of the bridel right anon.
210 And whan the hors was laus, he ginneth gon
Toward the fen, ther wilde mares renne,
And forth with 'wehee,' thurgh thikke and
      thurgh thenne.
   This millere gooth again, no word he seide,
But dooth his note, and with the clerkes pleyde,
Til that hir corn was faire and weel ygrounde.
And whan the mele is sakked and ybounde,
This John goth out and fint his hors away,
And gan to crie 'Harrow!' and 'Weylaway!
Oure hors is lorn, Alayn, for Goddes banes,

78

Step on thy feet! Com of, man, al atanes!   220
Allas, our wardeyn has his palfrey lorn.'
This Aleyn al forgat, bothe mele and corn;
Al was out of his minde his housbondrie.
'What, whilk way is he geen?' he gan to crie.
The wyf cam lepinge inward with a ren. *ran*
She seyde, 'Allas! youre hors goth to the fen *conspiring with Miller*
With wilde mares, as faste as he may go.
Unthank come on his hand that boond him so,
And he that bettre sholde han knit the reine!'
'Allas,' quod John, 'Aleyn, for Cristes peyne,   230
Lay doun thy swerd, and I wil myn alswa.
I is ful wight, God waat, as is a raa;
By Goddes herte, he sal nat scape us bathe!
Why ne had thow pit the capul in the lathe? *horse*
Ilhail! by God, Alayn, thou is a fonne!'
Thise sely clerkes han ful faste yronne *Keve Conspiring*
Toward the fen, bothe Aleyn and eek John. *with Miller*
And whan the millere saugh that they were gon,
He half a busshel of hir flour hath take,
And bad his wyf go knede it in a cake.   240
He seide, 'I trowe the clerkes were aferd.
Yet kan a millere make a clerkes berd,
For al his art; now lat hem goon hir weye!
Lo, wher he gooth! ye, lat the children pleye.
They gete him nat so lightly, by my croun.'
Thise sely clerkes rennen up and doun *watchword*
With 'Keep! keep! stand! stand! jossa, warderere,
Ga whistle thou, and I shal kepe him heere!'
But shortly, til that it was verray night,
They koude nat, though they dide al hir might,   250
Hir capul cacche, he ran alwey so faste,

Til in a dich they caughte him atte laste.
 Wery and weet, as beest is in the rein,
Comth sely John, and with him comth Aleyn.
'Allas,' quod John, 'the day that I was born!
Now are we drive til hething and til scorn.
Oure corn is stoln, men wil us fooles calle,
Bathe the wardeyn and oure felawes alle,
And namely the millere, weylaway!'
260 Thus pleyneth John as he gooth by the way
Toward the mille, and Bayard in his hond.
The millere sitting by the fyr he fond,
For it was night; and forther mighte they noght,
But for the love of God they him bisoght
Of herberwe and of ese, as for hir peny.
 The millere seide again, 'If ther be eny,
Swich as it is, yet shal ye have youre part.
Myn hous is streit, but ye han lerned art;
Ye konne by argumentes make a place
270 A mile brood of twenty foot of space.
Lat se now if this place may suffise,
Or make it rowm with speche, as is youre gise.'
 'Now, Simond,' seide John, 'by seint Cutberd,
Ay is thou myrie, and this is faire answerd.
I have herd seid, "man sal taa of twa thinges
Slik as he findes, or taa slik as he bringes."
But specially I pray thee, hooste deere,
Get us som mete and drinke, and make us cheere,
And we wil payen trewely atte fulle.
280 With empty hand men may na haukes tulle;
Loo, heere oure silver, redy for to spende.'
 This millere into toun his doghter sende
For ale and breed, and rosted hem a goos,

The Reeve's Tale

And boond hire hors, it sholde namoore go loos;
And in his owene chambre hem made a bed,
With sheetes and with chalons faire yspred
Noght from his owene bed ten foot or twelve.
His doghter hadde a bed, al by hirselve,
Right in the same chambre by and by.
It mighte be no bet, and cause why?
Ther was no roumer herberwe in the place.
They soupen and they speke, hem to solace,
And drinken evere strong ale atte beste.
Aboute midnight wente they to reste.

  Wel hath this millere vernisshed his heed;
Ful pale he was for dronken, and nat reed.
He yexeth, and he speketh thurgh the nose
As he were on the quakke, or on the pose.
To bedde he goth, and with him goth his wyf.
As any jay she light was and jolyf,   300
So was hir joly whistle wel ywet.
The cradel at hir beddes feet is set,
To rokken, and to yeve the child to sowke.
And whan that dronken al was in the crowke,
To bedde wente the doghter right anon;
To bedde goth Aleyn and also John;
Ther nas na moore, – hem nedede no dwale.
This millere hath so wisely bibbed ale
That as an hors he fnorteth in his sleep,
Ne of his tail bihinde he took no keep.   310
His wyf bar him a burdon, a ful strong;
Men mighte hir rowting heere two furlong;
The wenche rowteth eek, *par compaignye.*

  Aleyn the clerk, that herde this melodye,
He poked John, and seide, 'Slepestow?

Herdestow evere slik a sang er now?
Lo, swilk a complin is ymel hem alle,
A wilde fyr upon thair bodies falle!
Wha herkned evere slik a ferly thing?
320 Ye, they sal have the flour of il ending.
This lange night ther tides me na reste;
But yet, nafors, al sal be for the beste.
For, John,' seide he, 'als evere moot I thrive,
If that I may, yon wenche wil I swyve.
Som esement has lawe yshapen us;
For, John, ther is a lawe that says thus,
That gif a man in a point be agreved,
That in another he sal be releved.
Oure corn is stoln, sothly, it is na nay,
330 And we han had an il fit al this day;
And sin I sal have neen amendement
Again my los, I will have esement.
By Goddes sale, it sal neen other bee!'
   This John answerde, 'Alayn, avise thee!
The millere is a perilous man,' he seide,
'And gif that he out of his sleep abreyde,
He mighte doon us bathe a vileynye.'
   Aleyn answerde, 'I counte him nat a flye.'
And up he rist, and by the wenche he crepte.
340 This wenche lay uprighte, and faste slepte,
Til he so ny was, er she mighte espie,
That it had been to late for to crie,
And shortly for to seyn, they were aton.
Now pley, Aleyn, for I wol speke of John.
   This John lith stille a furlong wey or two,
And to himself he maketh routhe and wo.
'Allas!' quod he, 'this is a wikked jape;

82

The Reeve's Tale

Now may I seyn that I is but an ape.
Yet has my felawe somwhat for his harm;
He has the milleris doghter in his arm.   350
He auntred him, and has his nedes sped,
And I lie as a draf-sak in my bed;
And when this jape is tald another day,
I sal been halde a daf, a cokenay!
I wil arise and auntre it, by my faith!
"Unhardy is unseely," thus men saith.'
And up he roos, and softely he wente
Unto the cradel, and in his hand it hente,
And baar it softe unto his beddes feet.

Soone after this the wyf hir rowting leet,   360
And gan awake, and wente hire out to pisse,
And cam again, and gan hir cradel misse,
And groped heer and ther, but she foond noon.
'Allas!' quod she, 'I hadde almoost misgoon;
I hadde almoost goon to the clerkes bed.
Ey, benedicite! thanne hadde I foule ysped.'
And forth she gooth til she the cradel fond.
She gropeth alwey forther with hir hond,
And foond the bed, and thoghte noght but good,
By cause that the cradel by it stood,   370
And niste wher she was, for it was derk;
But faire and wel she creep in to the clerk,
And lith ful stille, and wolde han caught a sleep.
Withinne a while this John the clerk up leep,
And on this goode wyf he leith on soore.
So myrie a fit ne hadde she nat ful yoore;
He priketh harde and depe as he were mad.
This joly lyf han thise two clerkes lad
Til that the thridde cok bigan to singe.

380 Aleyn wax wery in the daweninge,
For he had swonken al the longe night,
And seide, 'Fare weel, Malyne, sweete wight!
The day is come, I may no lenger bide;
But everemo, wher so I go or ride,
I is thyn awen clerk, swa have I seel!'
    'Now, deere lemman,' quod she, 'go, far weel!
But er thow go, o thing I wol thee telle:
Whan that thou wendest homward by the melle,
Right at the entree of the dore bihinde
390 Thou shalt a cake of half a busshel finde
That was ymaked of thyn owene mele,
Which that I heelp my sire for to stele.
And, goode lemman, God thee save and kepe!'
And with that word almoost she gan to wepe.
    Aleyn up rist, and thoughte, 'Er that it dawe,
I wol go crepen in by my felawe';
And fond the cradel with his hand anon.
'By God,' thoughte he, 'al wrang I have misgon.
Myn heed is toty of my swink to-night,
400 That makes me that I ga nat aright.
I woot wel by the cradel I have misgo;
Heere lith the millere and his wyf also.'
And forth he goth, a twenty devel way,
Unto the bed ther as the millere lay.
He wende have cropen by his felawe John,
And by the millere in he creep anon,
And caughte him by the nekke, and softe he spak.
He seide, 'Thou John, thou swines-heed, awak,
For Cristes saule, and heer a noble game.
410 For by that lord that called is seint Jame,
As I have thries in this shorte night

84

Swyved the milleres doghter bolt upright,
Whil thow hast as a coward been agast.'
　'Ye, false harlot,' quod the millere, 'hast?
A, false traitour! false clerk!' quod he,
'Thow shalt be deed, by Goddes dignitee!
Who dorste be so boold to disparage
My doghter, that is come of swich linage?
And by the throte-bolle he caughte Alayn,
And he hente him despitously again,　　　　　　420
And on the nose he smoot him with his fest.
Doun ran the blody streem upon his brest;
And in the floor, with nose and mouth tobroke,
They walwe as doon two pigges in a poke;
And up they goon, and doun again anon,
Til that the millere sporned at a stoon,
And doun he fil bakward upon his wyf,
That wiste no thing of this nice stryf;
For she was falle aslepe a lite wight
With John the clerk, that waked hadde al night,　430
And with the fal out of hir sleep she breyde.
'Help! hooly crois of Bromeholm,' she seide,
'In manus tuas! Lord, to thee I calle!
Awak, Simond! the feend is on me falle.
Myn herte is broken; help! I nam but deed!
Ther lith oon upon my wombe and on myn heed.
Help, Simkin, for the false clerkes fighte!'
　This John stirte up as faste as ever he mighte,
And graspeth by the walles to and fro,
To finde a staf; and she stirte up also,　　　　440
And knew the estres bet than dide this John,
And by the wal a staf she foond anon,
And saugh a litel shimering of a light,

85

For at an hole in shoon the moone bright;
And by that light she saugh hem bothe two,
But sikerly she niste who was who,
But as she saugh a whit thing in hir ye,
And whan she gan this white thing espie,
She wende the clerk hadde wered a volupeer,
450 And with the staf she drow ay neer and neer,
And wende han hit this Aleyn at the fulle,
And smoot the millere on the piled skulle,
That doun he gooth, and cride, 'Harrow! I die!'
Thise clerkes beete him weel and lete him lie;
And greythen hem, and tooke hir hors anon,
And eek hire mele, and on hir wey they gon.
And at the mille yet they tooke hir cake
Of half a busshel flour, ful wel ybake.

Thus is the proude millere wel ybete,
460 And hath ylost the grindinge of the whete,
And payed for the soper everideel
Of Aleyn and of John, that bette him weel.
His wyf is swyved, and his doghter als.
Lo, swich it is a millere to be fals!
And therfore this proverbe is seid ful sooth,
'Him thar nat wene wel that yvele dooth';
A gilour shal himself bigiled be.
And God, that sitteth heighe in magestee,
Save al this compaignye, grete and smale!
470 Thus have I quit the Millere in my tale.

Heere is ended the Reves tale.

THE COOK'S PROLOGUE

The prologe of the Cokes Tale

The Cook of Londoun, whil the Reve spak,
For joye him thoughte he clawed him on the bak.
'Ha! ha!' quod he, 'for Cristes passion,
This millere hadde a sharp conclusion
Upon his argument of herbergage!
Wel seide Salomon in his langage,
"Ne bring nat every man into thyn hous";
For herberwinge by nighte is perilous.
Wel oghte a man avised for to be
Whom that he broghte into his privetee.   480
I pray to God, so yeve me sorwe and care
If evere, sithe I highte Hogge of Ware,
Herde I a millere bettre yset a-werk.
He hadde a jape of malice in the derk.
But God forbede that we stinte heere;
And therfore, if ye vouche-sauf to heere
A tale of me, that am a povre man,
I wol yow telle, as wel as evere I kan,
A litel jape that fil in oure citee.'
   Oure Hoost answerde and seide, 'I graunte it
      thee.   490
Now telle on, Roger, looke that it be good;
For many a pastee hastow laten blood,
And many a Jakke of Dovere hastow soold
That hath been twies hoot and twies coold.
Of many a pilgrim hastow Cristes curs,
For of thy percely yet they fare the wors,

That they han eten with thy stubbel goos;
For in thy shoppe is many a flye loos.
Now telle on, gentil Roger by thy name.
500 But yet I pray thee, be nat wroth for game;
A man may seye ful sooth in game and pley.'
    'Thou seist ful sooth,' quod Roger, 'by my fey!
But "sooth pley, quaad pley," as the Fleming seith.
And therfore, Herry Bailly, by thy feith,
Be thou nat wrooth, er we departen heer,
Though that my tale be of an hostileer.
But nathelees I wol nat telle it yit;
But er we parte, ywis, thou shalt be quit.'
And therwithal he lough and made cheere,
510 And seide his tale, as ye shul after heere.

THE COOK'S TALE

Heere biginneth the Cookes Tale.

A prentis whilom dwelled in oure citee,
And of a craft of vitailliers was hee.
Gaillard he was as goldfinch in the shawe,
Broun as a berye, a propre short felawe,
With lokkes blake, ykembd ful fetisly.
Dauncen he koude so wel and jolily
That he was cleped Perkin Revelour.
He was as ful of love and paramour
As is the hive ful of hony sweete:
Wel was the wenche with him mighte meete.   520
At every bridale wolde he singe and hoppe;
He loved bet the taverne than the shoppe.
For whan ther any riding was in Chepe,
Out of the shoppe thider wolde he lepe—
Til that he hadde al the sighte yseyn,
And daunced wel, he wolde nat come ayeyn—
And gadered him a meynee of his sort
To hoppe and singe and maken swich disport;
And ther they setten stevene for to meete,
To pleyen at the dys in swich a streete.   530
For in the toune nas ther no prentis
That fairer koude caste a paire of dys
Than Perkin koude, and therto he was free
Of his dispense, in place of privetee.
That fond his maister wel in his chaffare;
For often time he foond his box ful bare.
For sikerly a prentis revelour

That haunteth dys, riot, or paramour,
His maister shal it in his shoppe abye,
540 Al have he no part of the minstralcye.
For thefte and riot, they been convertible,
Al konne he pleye on giterne or ribible.
Revel and trouthe, as in a lowe degree,
They been ful wrothe al day, as men may see.
   This joly prentis with his maister bood
Til he were ny out of his prentishood,
Al were he snibbed bothe erly and late,
And somtime lad with revel to Newegate.
But atte laste his maister him bithoghte,
550 Upon a day, whan he his papir soghte,
Of a proverbe that seith this same word,
'Wel bet is roten appul out of hoord
Than that it rotie al the remenaunt.'
So fareth it by a riotous servaunt;
It is ful lasse harm to lete him pace,
Than he shende alle the servantz in the place.
Therfore his maister yaf him acquitance,
And bad him go, with sorwe and with meschance!
And thus this joly prentis hadde his leve.
560 Now lat him riote al the night or leve.
And for ther is no theef withoute a lowke,
That helpeth him to wasten and to sowke
Of that he bribe kan or borwe may,
Anon he sente his bed and his array
Unto a compeer of his owene sort,
That lovede dys, and revel, and disport,
And hadde a wyf that heeld for contenance
A shoppe, and swyved for hir sustenance.

NOTES

1. *folk*   i.e. the Canterbury pilgrims.
   this nice cas   i.e. the ludicrous events recounted in *The Miller's Tale* (see Introduction, pp. 6–8).
2. *hende*   In *The Miller's Tale* this term, a conventional epithet in popular romances, is repeatedly applied to Nicholas, the 'hero' of the tale. It has a wide range of meanings, including 'courteous', 'gentle', and 'handy' (i.e. both skilful and near at hand).
3. A similar line is used in three other *Canterbury Tales*. It is characteristic of Chaucer to allow for a variety of possible reactions to a particular story, rather than to insist that any one response is right.
6. *But it were*   'except'.
8–9. *A litel...a lite*   Ironic understatement, for the Reeve eventually shows more than a little anger against the Miller; though, characteristically, he largely represses the outward expression of his emotions.
9. *blamed it*   'found fault with the tale'.
10. Here the Reeve's introductory remarks begin, with the tale proper following at line 67. *So theek* 'so may I prosper', i.e. as I hope to prosper. An abbreviation of *so thee ik*, a northern form of an expression more commonly represented in Chaucer as *so theech*. It is used to give emphasis to a statement, by indicating that the speaker is fully committed to it; compare *als evere moot I thrive* in line 323.
11. 'With (a story of) the hoodwinking of a proud miller.'
13. *me list not pley for age*   'I don't care for frivolity because of my age.'
14. 'My time in the pasture is over: my nourishment is now dry winter food.' This is the first of a number of images that the Reeve takes from horses: he means that he has passed the springtime of his life, when he was like a horse cropping grass freely in the open air; now he is like a horse living on the dry unappetizing food of winter. Note the ingenious rhyme *for age/ forage*: rhyming on identical sounds with different meanings was an elegance practised by medieval French poets.

Notes

15. 'These white hairs of mine indicate my old age.'

16. *herte* The heart is here, as often, thought of as the source of sexual vigour. *Mowled* carries the unpleasant suggestion that the old man's white hairs are like mould growing on some decaying matter.

17. 'Unless it fares with me as with a medlar'. The medlar was popularly called an 'open-arse' because of its appearance. It was not thought ripe for eating until almost rotten.

18. *is ever lenger the wers* 'gets continually worse'; i.e. gets better to eat but worse in approaching rottenness; similarly, if a man's sexual interests and vigour increased with old age, that might be thought better from one point of view but worse from another.

19. *mullok...stree* This continues the ambiguity of the previous line: the medlar, approaching ripeness and rottenness at the same time, might be either thrown away on the rubbish-heap or carefully wrapped in protective straw. *Stree* recalls the earlier image of winter fodder.

22. 'So long as the world continues to play its music, we will continue to dance to it.' *The world* here implies the pleasures of this world as opposed to the next: so long as fleshly temptations offer themselves, old men cannot resist responding to them. The image of dancing is often associated in Chaucer with sexual activity: the Wife of Bath's 'olde daunce' (*General Prologue* 478) is that of love. Here he may be recalling the words of Jesus in Luke 7.32: 'They are like to children sitting in the market-place and speaking one to another and saying: We have piped to you and you have not danced; we have mourned and you have not wept.' *Hoppen* is an undignified word for 'dance', and implies that the old men make a ridiculous spectacle.

23. Like *herte*, *wil* is used here with special reference to sexual desires. The *nail* is a persistent longing, as sharp as a nail, and as firmly fixed in the will.

24-5. The leek, with its white root and green 'leaves', has to be inverted to make the comparison with an old man. The root then becomes his white head, and the tail his sexual parts, which he hopes will be green in the sense of youthfully vigorous.

28. 'There is still fire raked up in our ashes.' This completes the series of images of whiteness associated with old age: straw, white hair, mould, the leek, ashes.

29. The fire buried in ashes, which the line 28 suggested lust, is

Notes

now divided, as if by a preacher, into four other vices attributed to old age.

33. *ne...nat* As is common in Middle English, a negative may be doubled or even trebled for emphasis without implying a positive.

34. *a coltes tooth* Another horse image, presumably implying youthful appetites.

35. 'For all the many years that have passed away'.

36–41. The elaborate metaphor of these lines is taken from the wine-trade; Chaucer's father and grandfather were wine-merchants. When a medieval barrel of wine was to be drawn, it was laid on its side, and the *tappe*, the tapered stick used as a bung, was removed from its hole in one end. At first the wine would come spouting out vigorously, but as the level within the barrel dropped the stream would gradually decline to a mere trickle, which would splash down on to the *chymbe* or projecting rim immediately beneath it. The Reeve parallels this with the course of human life, and particularly sexuality; in his pessimistic view, the process of dying begins at the very moment of birth, and youthful vigour eventually gives way to mere talk.

36. *tappe* Used evidently to mean both the bung and the hole from which it is drawn. It does not of course mean a modern tap or faucet which can be turned on and off.

39. 'And the tap has been running like this ever since'.

42. A line of complex suggestion: the splashing of the last drops of wine suggests the babbling of the old man's tongue as he speaks of sinful behaviour in the past, and his tongue suggests the tongue or clapper of a bell, which rings and chimes with tedious repetitiveness, like the old man's talk.

44. 'There is nothing more left for old people, except this senile folly.'

45. *oure Hoost* i.e. the landlord of the Tabard Inn in Southwark, the organizer and 'master of ceremonies' of the pilgrimage and tale-telling competition. We learn his name at line 504.

47. *What amounteth al this wit?* 'What does all this wisdom amount to?'

48. *What shul* 'why must'.
hooly writ i.e. Scripture.

49–50. 'It was the devil who made a reeve preach, or turned a cobbler into a sailor or a doctor.'

51. *Sey forth* 'get on with telling'.

93

Notes

52–3. *Depeford...Grenewich* Places to the left of 'Watling Street', the route from Southwark to Canterbury. Deptford is about 6 km east of Southwark, and Greenwich about 11 km east. The progress of the pilgrimage is marked by a number of such references to places along the road.

52. *half-wey prime* Two methods of measuring time were current in the fourteenth century. The older method, that of the 'canonical' hours marked by the service bells of churches and monasteries, was based on a division of the period in which the sun was above the horizon into twelve 'hours', which therefore varied in length according to the time of year. This method had the advantage that the time of day could easily be roughly assessed if the sun could be seen; it was part of a whole way of life in which men's activities were governed by the sun and the seasons, and other, more exact methods of measuring time were unknown. By this method, *prime* was sunrise and the three 'hours' following it. The newer method was that familiar to us, by which the day is divided into twenty-four equal hours, which are of the same length whatever the time of year. This provided a more exact and convenient measurement of time, but, in the absence of a clock (and there were very few of these in England in Chaucer's time – probably no more than nine striking clocks in the whole country), it could be used only by rather complex calculations. By this method, *prime* meant 6 a.m. and the three following hours. Both methods are used at various points in *The Canterbury Tales*, but since there is no sign here that the Host has to make any calculation, we are presumably meant to understand that he simply glances at the sun and gives a rough estimate by the old method. The pilgrimage takes place in mid-April, which would correspond to a date near the end of April by our own calendar; and at this time of year halfway through canonical prime would be about 6.30 a.m. We are told in *The General Prologue* that the Host rose at dawn to put the pilgrims on the road without delay, and it is reasonable to suppose that they would have reached Deptford, riding slowly, by this time. For fuller discussion, see the article by Edward A. Block in *Speculum* XXXII (1957), to which we are much indebted.

53. *ther...inne* 'in which is many a scoundrel'. Greenwich does not really seem to have had a bad reputation; Chaucer is probably making a joke at his own expense, for it seems likely that he was living at Greenwich himself at the time when he wrote *The Reeve's Tale*.

54. *were þl* 'would be fully'. The subjunctive *were* is puzzling: it is probably ironically polite, as if the Host were saying, 'In view of all this, one might well think...'

57. *somdeel sette his howve* 'make him [the Miller] look a bit of a fool'. The underlying image is of someone coming up behind a man and twitching his hood over his eyes.

58. 'For it is permissible to repel force with force' – a well-known legal maxim, and one of a number of legal references in the tale. The Reeve's duties would require him to have some knowledge of law, but basic law was in any case a more familiar part of general knowledge in the Middle Ages than it is now.

59–60. It was the Miller's drunken condition that had caused him to insist on following the Knight as tale-teller, even though the Host had already called on the Monk to do so. He had made no attempt to conceal his condition, and had asked the pilgrims in advance to blame the Southwark ale for anything they might find offensive in his tale of how 'a clerk hath set the wrightes cappe' (a scholar deceived the carpenter).

61. In the portrait of the Reeve in *The General Prologue* we are told that he was a carpenter by trade; but the idea that *The Miller's Tale* was an attack on himself through his trade seems to be a product of the Reeve's own aggressive and suspicious imagination.

63. *cherles termes* Before repeating *The Miller's Tale*, Chaucer, in his role as pilgrim and reporter, had apologized for the fact that the Miller 'tolde his cherles tale in his manere' and that, being *cherles*, the Miller and the Reeve too told of *harlotrie* (low or dirty affairs). Both social and literary assumptions lie behind these references. In the class structure of medieval society, a *cherl* was a member of the lowest class, a peasant or workman; and, from the aristocratic standpoint of Chaucer's original public, only vulgar material and vulgar language could be expected of such a person. In rhetorical theory, the 'low' style and low genres such as the fabliau were associated with this class, even though written for and enjoyed by an aristocratic public. Here the Reeve is implying that he is a cut above the Miller socially, but that he will respond to his supposed attack in its own vulgar manner.

64. Here the Reeve's suppressed anger breaks out.

Notes

65–6. The Reeve is alluding to a saying from Jesus's Sermon on the Mount: 'And why seest thou the mote that is in thy brother's eye; and seest not the beam that is in thy own eye?' (Matthew 7.3). The images of the mote and the beam, or *balke* and *stalke*, refer to greater and lesser faults: the Reeve is accusing the Miller of hypocrisy or moral blindness in judging harshly the faults of others while disregarding his own.

THE REEVE'S TALE

67–9. Trumpington is a village some 4.5 km south of Cambridge. The river Cam divides near by into several streams. The precise site of the mill referred to cannot be determined, if indeed Chaucer had a specific site in mind, but it may have been at the place now called Byron's Pool. Chaucer may have owed his knowledge of the village and its mill to his acquaintance with Sir Roger de Trumpington.

69. *melle* This is a Kentish form of a word which Chaucer normally spells *mille*. A number of such forms are found in his work, presumably reflecting Kentish elements in his own brand of the London dialect of his time; this one is doubtless chosen for the rhyme with *telle* (as in lines 387–8), though it is appropriate to the Norfolk Reeve, for it was also common in East Anglia.

71. *was* i.e. had been.

72. The peacock, with its strutting gait and grandiose tail, is a traditional emblem of pride.

73. *Pipen* Since the pilgrim-Miller is represented in the *General Prologue* as playing a bagpipe, that is presumably the kind of pipe played by his counterpart in *The Reeve's Tale*.

fisshe A water-miller would naturally have fishing as a pastime and an additional means of sustenance.

74. *turne coppes* i.e. make wooden cups by turning them on a lathe.

wrastle The pilgrim-Miller, too, was a wrestler.

sheete i.e. shoot with bow and arrow (perhaps the water-fowl on the nearby marshes).

76. 'And it had the very sharp blade of a sword.' (A *panade* might have been a butcher's knife rather than a weapon.)

79. *Sheffeld thwitel* This is the first reference in English to Sheffield as a centre for the manufacture of cutlery; it is also the only occurrence in Chaucer of the word *thwitel*, a large knife.

96

Notes

Bennett mentions a number of fourteenth-century references to men being killed in brawls with *thwitels*.

81. *piled* The meaning of this word has been disputed, but, in view of lines 447–52, it presumably means 'bald'. Apes do not usually have bald skulls, but *camus* in the previous line also suggests an ape. Apes were traditionally associated with drunkenness and folly, both relevant qualities here.

82. *market-betere* This unusual word, found nowhere else in Chaucer, means someone who loafs around markets – evidently, in this miller's case, on the lookout for quarrels.

83–4. The double negative slightly confuses the meaning, in a way typical of colloquial utterance. A possible translation is: 'He swore that anyone who laid a hand upon him would pay for it, and so no man dared to do so.'

85. i.e. he stole both grain before it was ground and flour afterwards. That is why the two students later propose that one shall watch the grain go into the hopper above the mill, while the other watches the flour fall into the trough beneath.

86. *And that a sly* 'and a sly one too'.

87. This way of putting it deliberately makes it seem as though 'fiery' and 'scornful' are such notorious characteristics of the man as to be parts of his name. *Simkin* is a diminutive of 'Simon' (cf. line 168).

89. Medieval priests were of course not permitted to marry or have children; hence the contemptuous irony of *noble* in the preceding line. Simkin's wife was illegitimate, and her birth was nothing to be proud of, though in reality it was not uncommon for such situations to occur. Bennett points out that earlier in the century a real parson of Trumpington had had a bastard who succeeded him as parish priest!

90. The brass pans, for cooking, were given with her as a dowry, to persuade the evidently wealthy miller to marry her.

91. 'So that Simkin should marry into his family.' There may be a pun on another sense of *allye*, meaning 'alloy': brass is an alloy, a cheap metal superficially resembling the noble gold, and this might suggest that the marriage alliance was an alloy of the same kind.

92. One of the functions of medieval nunneries was to provide a genteel upbringing for girls whose parents could afford to pay for it.

94. *But* 'unless'.

97

95. 'In order to preserve his position as a yeoman.' A yeoman was a respectable commoner, above the rank of a *cherl* but below that of a gentleman.

96. *peert as is a pye* A traditional comparison; and the line's alliteration adds to its jaunty effect.

97. 'The pair of them made a really fine sight.'

98. *halydayes* i.e. the special feast-days of the Church, which were both holy days and holidays.

99. *tipet* a long piece trailing from the hood, like a scarf.

100. *gyte of reed* The exact meaning of *gyte* is uncertain: probably a robe. In the Middle Ages, when distinctions of social rank were marked by legally enforceable distinctions of dress, it was forbidden for someone of the rank of a miller's wife to wear scarlet. There are many contemporary complaints about the breaking of such rules, but the red robe is here part of the picture of social pride.

101. *of the same* i.e. to match.

102. 'There was no-one who dared call her anything but "my lady".'

103–4. 'There was no passer-by so bold as to dare to flirt or even joke with her.'

108. 'At least they wish that their wives should imagine so.'

109. *smoterlich* i.e. sullied in reputation (because of her illegitimate birth). It is characteristic of Chaucer's shrewd observation that he should tell us that she was all the more arrogant *because* of her shady origin, not despite it.

110. The mocking alliterative comparison of pride to stagnant ditchwater (they both keep people at a distance) is traditional, but it is particularly appropriate to the fenny setting of the tale.

111. *hoker . . . bisemare* 'disdain . . . scorn'. These words are used nowhere else in Chaucer; they are commonly paired together in Middle English homiletic writings, and we may think of them as belonging to the Reeve's own moralizing vocabulary.

112. *Hir thoughte* 'it seemed to her (that)'.

116. *withouten any mo* 'and no more [children]'.

117. *of half yeer age* 'six months old'.

118. *a propre page* 'a fine lad' – a colloquial expression.

119. *wenche* A word applied only to lower-class or disreputable young women.

120. She has her father's snub nose, but the glass-grey eyes that are a conventional feature of the heroine of medieval romance.

Notes

Greye as glas is a common alliterative phrase. Colour-words are often not very exact in Middle English, and possibly the colour intended is the blue-green of thick glass, there being no virtually colourless glass in the Middle Ages.

121. Another incongruous combination of the country girl (broad buttocks) and the romance heroine (round, high breasts). The alliterative linking underlines the absurdity; in this context it may have suggested provinciality to Chaucer and his audience. (The Parson in his Prologue associates alliterative verse with the north.)

122. The *But* speaks volumes: apparently defending her beauty with a reference to its crowning glory, it actually concedes that it was her only really attractive feature. *I wol nat lie* is an empty assertion of a kind often found in popular romance; it helps to place the girl in an appropriately banal setting. *Fair* probably means 'beautiful', but since blonde hair was much admired in medieval ladies, it may well imply the colour too.

125. His *catel* is his moveable property, his *mesuage* is his dwelling-house and the land on which it was built: more legal terminology, such as a reeve might be expected to be familiar with.

127. *bistowe hire hye* 'marry her well'.

128. 'Into some respectable family of good descent'.

129–32. These lines, purporting to explain and justify the parson's intention, are meant ironically, and constitute a sharp attack on his moral blindness, as is made clear by the increasingly contemptuous repetition of *hooly, chirche,* and *blood,* and by the savage final word *devoure.* The true *good* of *hooly chirche* is not property but virtue; and the phrase *hooly blood* is more commonly used to refer to the blood of Christ, shed to redeem mankind, than to a priest's illegitimate granddaughter.

130. 'On blood which is that of Holy Church by direct descent', i.e. on the parson's granddaughter.

132. 'Even if he had to swallow up Holy Church to do it' (by misapplying ecclesiastical property to create a large dowry for his granddaughter).

133. *sokene* The right of the mill to grind the corn of the inhabitants of the district, and the miller's right to receive payment for doing so (see Introduction, p. 38).

134. *whete and malt* The wheat was used primarily for making bread; the malt was ground from barley to make ale. Different types of stone were needed to grind the two kinds of grain.

136. 'Which people call the "Soler Hall" at Cambridge.' It is generally agreed that this refers to the King's Hall, then the largest of the Cambridge colleges (it has now been absorbed into Trinity); but there is no record of its having been called by this name. Some manuscripts read *Scoler Halle*, which would presumably mean 'hall of scholars', but it is perhaps more likely that this represents the attempt of medieval scribes to make sense of an unfamiliar expression. The buildings of the King's Hall did have an unusually large number of 'solars' or upper rooms; and since two Oxford academic halls *were* called 'Soler Hall', it may be either that the King's Hall was so called colloquially but not officially (hence *men clepen*) or that Chaucer was mingling Oxford and Cambridge references. For discussion see Bennett, pp. 93–7, and D. S. Brewer in *Chaucer Review* v (1970–1).

138. *in a stounde*   It is uncertain whether this is to be taken with the previous statement, as meaning 'on one occasion, for a period' (as in line 153), or whether it goes with the next line and means 'in an attack (of illness)'.

139. *maunciple*   The college officer whose duty it was to supply the members with provisions.

143. *but curteisly*   'only with discretion'. The miller's 'courtesy' amounts only to keeping his theft within discreet limits.

145. *wardeyn*   This title for the head of a college was and is commoner at Oxford than at Cambridge, but the head of the King's Hall was called *custos* (warden) in the fourteenth century.

146. 'But the miller didn't care a scrap [literally, a weed] about that.' *Tare* was a common expression for something valueless, but it is particularly appropriate for a man who must be on the lookout for weeds among the corn.

148. 'Poor scholars' is virtually a formula. In *The Reeve's Tale* the scholars' poverty has no special significance, though it is of some importance in the closest French analogue, where they have to turn bakers in order to avoid starvation. Indeed, since these scholars are later able to offer silver for a night's lodging, they are presumably quite well off. In a modern college, a 'scholar' would be an undergraduate, but Aleyn and John may well be young fellows of their college.

150. *lusty for to pleye*   'eager for amusement'.

152. 'They eagerly entreat the warden.'

155. 'And they dared boldly wager their lives [literally, necks]'.

Notes

156–7. *stele hem...by sleighte, ne by force hem reve* 'steal from them by cunning nor snatch from them by force'. This ABCCBA order (here, verb–pronoun–adverbial phrase–adverbial phrase–pronoun–verb) is a neat example of the rhetorical figure of chiasmus; even the style of fabliau can have a concealed elegance.

half a pekke i.e. one gallon (about 4.5 litres), corn being measured by volume.

160. *Strother* A northern place-name, though the particular town or village cannot be identified.

161. This dismissive attitude to the north prepares us for the 'barbarous' dialect the young men speak.

164. *clerk* In the earlier Middle Ages, learning, and even literacy, had been largely confined to the clergy; hence in Chaucer's time a *clerk* still meant both an ecclesiastic, or cleric (including one in minor orders, such as a deacon), and a scholar or student. Aleyn and John are probably not priests, and may be destined for secular office (because the King's Hall was founded by Edward II in order to provide recruits for the civil service), but they wear the tonsure and should in theory be celibate.

168–70. The students and the miller evidently know each other already, since they are on Christian-name terms. This implies some kind of background to the contest between them, and line 169 suggests that Aleyn has noticed the attractions of the wife and daughter on a previous visit and also prepares us for the part they are to play on this occasion.

169. *fares* The -(e)s ending for verbs in the plural or the third person singular is a northernism.

172. *nede has na peer* 'necessity has no equal', i.e. there is nothing like necessity for making one do something. Note that *has*, the standard form in modern English, was a northernism in the fourteenth century; Chaucer's normal form is *hath*.

173. 'He who has no servant must serve himself.' This probably, and *nede has na peer* certainly, are traditional sayings rather than (as the following line suggests) learned ones, though they may have been transmitted through Latin proverb-collections.

175. *Hope* still has the older meaning of 'expect' as well as its modern meaning. The ambiguity adds to the general impression of comic clumsiness of speech.

176. *wanges* Probably a northern word for 'back teeth', though

it has been suggested that it could mean the sides of the face or temples. Death expected from toothache seems appropriate to a comic tale.

177. *is I come* 'I have come'. Verbs of motion are often conjugated with 'to be' in Chaucer's English, but *is* is a northernism for *am*.

179. Literally, 'I beg you to hasten us hence as [fast as] you can'. *Heythen* is a northern form of *henne* (as in line 35). Note the change from the singular *thy* of Aleyn's initial jaunty greeting (169) to the politer plural *yow* and *ye* of this request.

182. *hopur* 'hopper', the inverted cone above the mill-stones into which the grain is poured for grinding. It is so called because it 'hops' or shakes up and down (*wagges til and fra*, 185) with the motion of the heavy stones below it.

184. *Yet saugh I nevere* 'I have never previously seen'.
by my fader kin 'by my father's family' – a common oath, in an age when ancestry was of great importance, but particularly appropriate here in view of what we have been told about the miller's obsession with matters of descent.

186. *wiltow swa?* Literally, 'wilt thou so?', i.e. 'is that what you intend?'

187. *by my croun* A common oath, with 'crown' standing for 'head' and hence for 'life'. But Aleyn may possibly be referring more specifically to his tonsure, the outward mark of his clerkly status, since the contest in the tale is not just between individuals but between two clerks and a miller.

190. *I may been of youre sort* 'I may be said to be a person of your type.'

190–1. The explanation sounds contrived, and suggests that Aleyn and John have arranged it in advance, so as to have an excuse for watching both grain and flour. The following speech shows that Simkin sees through their plan.

193. *nis doon but for a wile* 'is only done for a trick'.

195. *by my thrift* 'as I hope to prosper' – again a common oath, but one particularly appropriate to its context, since it is by successful dishonesty that the miller has prospered so far.
blere hir ye cf. line 11.

196. *philosophye* Popularly used to refer to academic learning generally.

201. Yet another horse image: this refers to a widespread fable in which the wolf asks the mare if he can buy her foal (to eat). In

Notes

Caxton's fifteenth-century version, the mare replies that if he 'conne rede and be a clerk' he can read the price written on her hoof; but when the wolf tries to look at it she kicks him. The fox draws the moral that 'the beste clerkes ben not the wisest men'.

202. 'I don't care a scrap for all their "art"' (cf. line 146). *Art* combines two meanings: the arts course which the miller supposes the two students to be following at Cambridge, and learning or cunning or 'artfulness' in a more general sense.

206. *ther as* 'where'.

208. *goth him faire and wel* 'goes neatly and easily'. *Faire and wel* is a formula (cf. lines 215 and 372). The redundant reflexive pronoun *him* gives an effect of greater familiarity or intimacy.

212. *wehee* A whinny, usually associated with sexual desire.
thurgh thikke and thurgh thenne A still-current alliterative formula; perhaps, when applied to a fen, it might be translated 'through wet and dry'. *Thenne* is a Kentish form, used for the rhyme.

219. *for Goddes banes* 'for God's sake [literally, "bones"]'.

220. 'Get moving! Come along, man, this very moment!' *Step on thy feet* is no doubt meant to sound a ridiculously provincial expression.

221. *palfrey* A small horse for everyday riding, as opposed to a warhorse or carthorse. Evidently they had borrowed the horse from the warden of their college; heads of colleges were often allowed a horse at the college's expense, whereas junior members were not permitted to keep one.

222. *al forgat* 'forgot everything'.

224. *geen* If this is not a scribe's mistake, it must be meant as a northernism.

228–9. 'May a curse come on the hand of the man who tied him up like that, and who ought to have fastened the rein better!'

230–5. In his excitement, John's northern dialect gets even thicker.

230. *for Cristes peyne* 'for the sake of Christ's passion'.

234. *ne had* Probably pronounced 'nad'.

239. *half a busshel* i.e. 4 gallons, or about 18 litres.

242. *make a clerkes berd* 'outwit a scholar'. The underlying image is of trimming someone's beard for him.

243. *art* cf. line 202 and note.
lat hem goon hir weye 'let them follow their own devices'.

244. *he* i.e. the horse.

103

245. *gete him nat* 'won't get him'.

    by my croun cf. line 187 and note. We are perhaps meant to remember the miller's *piled...skulle* (81): the crown of his head is as hairless as that of the students.

251. *capul cacche* The northern word *capul* (horse) is here used by the storyteller, either in imitation of the students (at line 234) or because for Chaucer it belonged to vulgar speech generally. It may be just by accident that the alliterative phrase recalls alliterative poetry, in which *capul* is used not as a vulgarism but as a poetic term.

258. *felawes* 'companions, comrades'. But in a college context the word has a more specialised meaning, and that may be intended here, especially in view of the juxtaposition with *wardeyn*.

261. *Bayard* A name for a bay-coloured horse, but probably also incorporating a mock-heroic allusion to the magic steed of that name given in French romance by Charlemagne to one of his heroes. The name often implies recklessness, and that would be appropriate here.

262–5. The contrast between the bedraggled students, and the miller sitting in complacent comfort by the fire, is particularly galling for them; yet they have no choice but to beg him for overnight lodging, because after dark they would be locked out of Cambridge, which, like other medieval towns, was enclosed. Bennett suggests that Trumpington had no inn.

263. *forther mighte they noght* 'they could go no further'. In Middle English a verb of motion can be omitted after an auxiliary if the meaning is clear without it.

265. *herberwe and...ese* 'lodging and refreshment'. The two words are often used as a pair.

    as for hir peny 'in return for payment'.

266. *seide again* 'replied'.

268–72. Simkin crowns his triumph over the students with some heavy irony at the expense of their academic studies. The medieval arts course included logic, and the passage alludes to the propensity of academic philosophers to 'prove' truths that do not correspond to, or that even contradict, common human experience. The fourteenth-century universities seemed to contemporaries to be particularly open to such accusations. Space and narrowness will be especially important in the second half of the story.

Notes

269. *argumentes*   This was a more technical term in Chaucer's time than now, implying here something like 'processes of abstract reasoning'.

271. *Lat se now*   'now let us see'.

273. *seint Cutberd*   A northern saint, whose body is buried in Durham cathedral.
Cutberd (cut-beard) is no doubt intended as a comic mispronunciation.

274. 'You are always joking, and that is a clever answer.' John has no choice but to flatter the miller if he and Aleyn are to spend a tolerable night.

275–6. 'A man must take one of two things – what he finds, or what he brings with him.' A proverbial saying, which will turn out to have an unexpected application, since the two students do indeed take what they find.

278. *make us cheere*   'give us a warm welcome'.

280. 'One cannot entice hawks with an empty hand.' Another proverb: hawks, kept for hunting, were trained to come to hand by being offered food, and were notorious for responding only to this material inducement. The comparison is not much to Simkin's advantage; but since the hawk has aristocratic associations it may have pleased his snobbery.

282. *into toun*   'into the village'. If the mill was at Byron's Pool, that is some way outside Trumpington itself. Presumably there was an alehouse, even if nowhere that offered lodgings.

284. *it sholde*   'so that it should'.

286. *chalons*   'blankets' – so called from Chalons in France, where they were made.

290. *cause why?*   'for what reason?'

292. *hem to solace*   'to entertain themselves'.

293. *drinken evere*   'keep on drinking'.

295. *vernisshed his heed*   Literally, 'varnished his head', a colloquial expression for getting drunk. It can be taken almost literally here: his bald head gets shiny with perspiration, and that is no doubt one reason why it reflects the moonlight later.

296. *for dronken*   'through drunkenness'.

298. 'As if he were suffering from hoarseness or a cold'.

300. The jay, a brightly coloured, chattering bird, is a traditional comparison for empty-headedness.

301. 'To wet one's whistle' is still a colloquial phrase for having

a drink. The alliteration, underlining the emphatic rhythm, gives the line a rollicking effect.

303. *to yeve the child to sowke* 'so that the child could be breast-fed'.

304. 'And when everything in the jug was drunk'.

307. *Ther nas na moore* 'That was all there was to it.'

308. *wisely* Ironic, of course.

309. Note the further horse comparison.

310. *tail* This continues the horse image, but is also a vulgar word for the human behind.

311. 'His wife provided him with a refrain, a very powerful one.' The 'music' in question is that of their snores and snorts.

312. *two furlong* 440 yards (about 400 metres).

313. *par compaignye* The polite French phrase is particularly ridiculous in its context.

317. *complin* Continuing the music image, Aleyn refers to their threefold snoring as their 'compline' or evening service.

318. 'May erysipelas [a painful skin disease] attack their bodies!' Though *thair* resembles the standard modern form, in Chaucer's time it was a northernism for his normal word, *hir* (as in line 312).

320. *the flour of il ending* 'the best of a bad end'. This amusingly paradoxical phrase brings together several meanings for *flour*: see Introduction, p. 40.

323. *als evere moot I thrive* 'as I may ever prosper'.

325. 'The law has provided us with some redress.' This *esement* (a legal term) may make us think of the *ese* the students begged at line 265; it will indeed prove to be refreshment to them as well as redress.

327–8. 'That if a man is injured in one respect, he shall be granted remedy in another'. There was a legal maxim to this effect. Aleyn could have been studying law at the King's Hall, which had many law books in its library. *Releved*, besides having this legal sense, can also refer more generally to gaining relief (for example, for a physical urge); both senses are relevant to Aleyn's intentions.

329. *it is na nay* 'there is no denying it'.

331–2. *sin I sal...my los* 'since I shall not receive any amends in respect of my loss'.

333. *it sal neen other bee* 'it shall not be otherwise'.

337. *vileynye* The sort of act to be expected of a *vileyn*, or peasant.

Notes

342. *had been to late* 'would have been too late'. The soothing explanation leaves us to speculate about her real response.

344. *pley* 'enjoy yourself'. The unexpected shift from Aleyn to John seems tactful, but turns out to introduce a surprising development in the plot.

345. *a furlong wey or two* 'for as long as it would take to walk 200 or 400 metres'.

346. 'And he laments and grumbles to himself'.

347. *wikked jape* 'rotten trick'.

348. *ape* i.e. dupe.

349. 'My pal has at least got something back for his injury.'

351. 'He took the risk, and has prospered in his affairs.'

352. *draf-sak* 'sack of draff'. Draff is rubbish, especially husks; a real sack of it might well be found in a mill, but 'draff-sack' was also used figuratively to mean a lazy glutton, which would be equally appropriate here.

356. *Unhardy is unseely* 'The cowardly man is unfortunate.' The equivalent modern proverb is 'Nothing venture, nothing win.'

361. *hire* A redundant reflexive pronoun.

362. *gan* Probably used here, as often, as an auxiliary verb to indicate the past tense.

366. *benedicite* Pronounced as if spelt 'bendistee'.
hadde I foule ysped 'I would have prospered badly', i.e. things would have gone badly with me.

367–79. In this passage, with its tension and its account of minute details in temporal sequence, there is a particularly striking mixture of the present tense with the past – a narrative equivalent to the cinematic close-up.

369. *thoughte noght but good* 'thought nothing but that all was well'.

373. *caught a sleep* 'fallen asleep'.

375. *goode wyf* The two words are conventionally associated to mean 'housewife' or 'lady of the house'. Here *goode* has ironic reverberations, though the miller's wife evidently does not realize that it is not her husband in bed with her. The second *on* is redundant.

376. 'She had not had such a pleasant bout for a very long time.'

379. *the thridde cok* Cocks were said to crow three times, the first at midnight and the third just before dawn.

382–93. A traditional part of the medieval courtly romance is the *aube*, the parting exchange between lovers as dawn separates them. These speeches represent a lower-class parody of the courtly convention, in which the lover's traditional reluctance to depart is replaced by weariness and the lady's offering of a pledge becomes the disclosure of the whereabouts of the stolen flour. See R. E. Kaske in *English Literary History* XXVI (1959).

382. *Malyne*   This is probably the same name as 'Malkin', a diminutive of Maud or Matilda. It is frequently used in Middle English as a name for a lower-class woman, generally with the implication of sluttishness: thus the Host elsewhere speaks of how lost time will not return any more than 'Malkynes maidenhede'. As a common noun, *malkin* meant 'dish-mop', and that association may also be present.

384. *go or ride*   'walk or ride' – a formula implying any sort of motion.

385. *swa have I seel!*   'as I may have salvation!', i.e. 'as I hope to be saved!'

386. *lemman*   'sweetheart', a word with vulgar associations.

389. *dore bihinde*   'back door'.

392. *that*   Redundant.

398. *al wrang I have misgon*   'I have gone badly astray'.

399. *toty of*   'dizzy from'. This is the only occurrence of *toty* in Chaucer.

403. *a twenty devel way*   'as if twenty devils were after him'.

405. *wende have cropen*   'intended to have crept'.

408. *swines-heed*   Implying lazy self-indulgence.

410. There seems to be no special significance in this choice of saint; and *that lord that called is* is probably added as a metrical filler.

411. *As*   Introduces an assertion, something sworn to be true.

417–18. The miller's pride in his family, unmentioned for so long, is reintroduced with special force at this climax. He is concerned not that his daughter has been seduced, but that her seducer is of low social rank.

417. *to disparage*   'as to dishonour'; specifically, *disparage* is to degrade by making an unequal match.

420–2. The *he* of line 420 is presumably Aleyn, but it is not clear who punches whose nose in lines 421–2. In the circumstances, the confusion is lifelike.

421. *fest*   Another Kentish form, used for the rhyme.

424. 'Pig in a poke' is still a current alliterative phrase, referring

to something bought unseen, but whether piglets were really sold in bags we do not know.

432. *hooly crois of Bromeholm* Near Bromholm in Norfolk was the priory of St Andrew, which was supposed to possess a piece of the true Cross, and was therefore the goal of many pilgrimages. The East Anglian reference is appropriate to the Reeve.

433. *In manus tuas* 'into thy hands' – a well known formula, appropriate to someone supposed on the point of death, since it alludes to the last words of Jesus on the Cross: 'Into thy hands I commend my spirit' (Luke 23.46).

434. Half-asleep, she imagines she has been attacked by an incubus, a devil that was supposed to sleep with women and get them pregnant.

435. *nam but* 'am' (literally, 'am nothing but').

439. 'And groped back and forth along the walls'.

441. *estres* i.e. the interior arrangements.

444. Evidently the bedroom has no window; glass was still very expensive in Chaucer's time.

447. *in hir ye* 'with her eye'. The implication is that she caught only a glimpse of it.

460. That is, he was not paid for his work in grinding the wheat.

464. 'You see, that's what happens when a miller is dishonest!'

465-7. A proverb or *sententia* is one way in which medieval works on rhetoric recommend that a poem should be brought to an end.

466. 'He who does evil need not expect [to receive] good.'

467. Another proverb.

468-9. Many of the tales end in this way, with a formal blessing.

THE COOK'S PROLOGUE

472. Literally, 'The pleasure it gave him made it seem as if he was scratching his back'. To scratch someone's back is often used to mean to do him a benefit or pleasure, or to flatter him, as in the saying, 'You scratch my back and I'll scratch yours'. Here it is not quite clear whose back is being scratched, but probably the line implies that the Reeve's story so delighted the Cook that it gave him an almost sensory pleasure.

473. *for Cristes passion* 'by Christ's suffering'. Compare John's oath, 'for Cristes peyne' (230). Such oaths are over-emphatic and evidently, in Chaucer's eyes, vulgar, since he almost invariably puts them on the lips of lower-class characters.

Notes

474–5. 'This miller suffered a painful outcome to his disputation about lodgings.' The remark looks back to the miller's joke about *argumentes* and constricted lodgings at 263–72. The following lines make clear the Cook's implication: the miller thought he was getting the better of the students by making them lodge for the night at his house, but the reverse turned out to be the case. *Conclusion*, like *argument*, is a semi-technical term from the scholastic philosophy of the Middle Ages: here they are appropriate to the university setting of *The Reeve's Tale*, but are used ironically, since the conflict between the miller and the students was settled not verbally but physically.

477. Compare Ecclesiasticus 11.31: 'Bring not every man into thy house: for many are the snares of the deceitful.' Ecclesiasticus, which is relegated to the Apocrypha of the Anglican Bible, is here wrongly attributed to the wise king Solomon, supposed author of the other wisdom-literature of Scripture.

479–80. 'A man ought to take careful thought over whom he brings into his private dwelling.' *Avised* means 'advised', either by someone else or by one's own thoughts. There is probably a pun on *privetee*, which, as in *The Miller's Tale*, can mean the private parts of a woman as well as other private things. By forcing the students to spend the night in his house, the miller has brought about the dishonouring of his wife and daughter.

481. *so yeve me* 'may I be given'.

482. *sithe I highte Hogge of Ware* i.e. 'since I was christened'. Ware is in Hertfordshire, and is here used, as place-names often were, as a surname. There appears to have been a real cook named Roger Ware in the late fourteenth century; a number of the Canterbury pilgrims were probably based on real persons.

484. *hadde a jape of malice* 'was the victim of a malicious trick'.

487. *of me* 'from me'.

489. *oure citee* i.e. London.

492. To 'let blood' or 'bleed' (i.e. to remove some of the blood from the veins) was a recognized remedy for many ailments. The implication is presumably that Roger's unsold meat-pies had had the gravy removed to make them keep longer, and therefore looked dry and pale.

493. *Jakke of Dovere* Probably a reheated pie, which would be likely to give food-poisoning to anyone who ate it.

495. *Cristes curs* i.e. a curse sworn 'by Christ'.

496. 'They are still the worse because of your parsley.' The implication is that there had been flies among the parsley used to stuff the goose.

497. *stubbel goos* A goose fatted by being fed on stubble.

499. *by thy name* 'as you are called'. The Host's insistence on the Cook's name may indicate Chaucer's determination to expose the real Roger of Ware as the object of his satire. *Gentil* is of course used ironically: the Cook is noble neither by birth nor by nature.

500. *for game* 'on account of a joke'.

501. Proverbial – compare 'Many a true word is spoken in jest.' Thus the Host retracts what had seemed the soothing effect of his previous line.

503. *Sooth pley, quaad pley* 'A true joke is a bad joke.' There was really a Flemish proverb to this effect, which Chaucer is likely to have known through contacts with some of the Flemish traders in London.

504. A real Harry Bailly was an innkeeper in Southwark in Chaucer's time.

505–6. Chaucer seems to have planned to repeat, as a motive for *The Cook's Tale*, the hostility between pilgrims that had provoked the Reeve to tell a tale against the Miller. As in the previous case, the hostility has a professional basis, since there was competition between cooks and innkeepers as to which had the right to provide travellers with food.

THE COOK'S TALE

511–12. i.e., he was apprenticed to a master who belonged to a gild or association of victuallers. In the Middle Ages, the various trades were organized and controlled by associations of masters, who laid down the conditions of apprenticeship, standards of craftsmanship, prices, etc.

513. Goldfinches are brightly coloured and sing gaily.

514. *Broun as a berye* A traditional alliterative formula: it may imply that he had a dark or reddish-brown complexion, but it is possible that *broun* retains one of its older senses, as 'bright', implying a bright red or apple-cheeked appearance.

517. *Perkin Revelour* 'Pete the merry-maker'.

520. 'It was lucky for [literally, it was well with] the girl who might meet with him'.

523. *Chepe* Cheapside, a major shopping street in London, and a favourite place for processions.

527. 'And collected together a gang of lads of his type.'

528. *maken swich disport* 'have fun of that kind'.

532. *fairer* 'more neatly' – the word does not imply that he did not cheat.

534. *place of privetee* 'a private place'. In view of the earlier puns on *privetee*, the phrase may carry a vague suggestion of immoral purposes.

535–6. 'His master [i.e. the victualler to whom he was apprenticed] easily discovered that in his trading, for many a time he found his cash-box completely empty.' The apprentice used his master's money for his own shady purposes.

539. The word *it* refers back to the whole situation indicated in the first two lines of the sentence: thus, 'For certainly, if he has a merry-making apprentice,...the master shall suffer for it in his workplace...'.

540. 'Although he enjoys no share of the minstrelsy' – i.e., though he pays the piper, he does *not* call the tune.

541. i.e. dissipation and theft are different words for the same thing.

542. 'It doesn't matter if he plays on the gittern (a zither-like instrument) or the fiddle.'

543–4. 'In a person of low rank, merry-making and honesty are always incompatible [literally, angry], as may be seen.' A man of high rank might be wealthy enough to finance his own dissipation; a mere apprentice would be bound to pay for his revelry by dishonest means.

545. It was normal for apprentices to live in their masters' houses, as members of the family.

546. *were* 'was'. (The subjunctive is commonly used in clauses introduced by *til*, though its use where the verb is in the past tense, as here, is less common.) An apprentice would be bound to his master for a fixed term of years.

547. 'Although he was constantly scolded'. *Bothe erly and late* is a common tag meaning 'at all times'.

548. People being taken to prison in London were really sometimes accompanied by minstrels, to call attention to their disgrace; here we are no doubt meant to compare this *revel* with the *revel* that caused Perkin to be imprisoned. There is possibly even a double meaning in *lad with revel*: both 'taken with merry-making' and 'led by [his own] merry-making'.

550. *his papir soghte* 'was looking through his accounts' (and

presumably finding further evidence of his apprentice's dishonesty).

551. *this same word*   i.e. 'as follows'.

554. *So fareth it by*   'it is the same with'.

556. *Than he shende*   'than that he should spoil'.

559–60. Another example of the rhyming of identical words with different meanings: *leve* means first 'permission to depart' and then 'leave off'.

562–3. 'Who helps him to extract and consume whatever he is able to steal or borrow'.

564. *his bed*   i.e. his bedding, which would be his own, portable possession.

567. *for contenance*   'to keep up appearances'.

568. *for hir sustenance*   'to support herself'.

SUGGESTIONS FOR FURTHER READING

Of the comparatively small amount of discussion of *The Reeve's Tale* that has been published in book form, the following will probably be found the most useful:

J. A. W. Bennett, *Chaucer at Oxford and at Cambridge* (Clarendon Press, 1974)
Derek Brewer, 'The Fabliaux' in *Companion to Chaucer Studies*, ed. Beryl Rowland (Oxford University Press, Toronto, 1968)
T. W. Craik, *The Comic Tales of Chaucer* (Methuen, 1964)
R. W. V. Elliott, *Chaucer's English* (André Deutsch, 1974)
Charles Muscatine, *Chaucer and the French Tradition* (University of California Press, 1957)

Parallel material of various kinds will be found in Chaucer's other fabliaux (especially *The Miller's Tale*) and in:

The Literary Context of Chaucer's Fabliaux, ed. Larry D. Benson and Theodore M. Andersson (Indiana University Press, 1971)
Medieval Comic Tales, trans. Peter Rickard et al. (D. S. Brewer, 1972)

Those to whom scholarly periodicals are available will find it helpful to consult:

M. Copland, 'The *Reeve's Tale* – Harlotrie or Sermonyng?', *Medium Aevum* XXXI (1962), 14–32
G. F. Jones, 'Chaucer and the Medieval Miller', *Modern Language Quarterly* XVI (1955), 3–15
R. E. Kaske, 'An Aube in *The Reeve's Tale*', *English Literary History* XXVI (1959), 295–310
Ian Lancashire, 'Sexual Innuendo in the *Reeve's Tale*', *Chaucer Review* VI (1971–2), 159–70
Glending Olson, 'The *Reeve's Tale* as a Fabliau', *Modern Language Quarterly* XXXV (1974), 219–30
Paul A. Olson, '*The Reeve's Tale*: Chaucer's *Measure for Measure*', *Studies in Philology* LIX (1962), 1–17

GLOSSARY

The mark (N) against an entry indicates that it is a northern word or form.

abegge (N) (inf. *abeggen*) pay for it

aboute about; round; around

abreyde (inf. *abreyden*) awake

abye (inf. *abyen*) pay for, suffer for

acquitance release

adoun down

aferd frightened

after after; behind; afterwards, next

again again; back; in return; (l. 331) in respect of

agast terrified

agreved (inf. *agreven*) injured

al all; completely, fully; everything; although

alday all day

Aleyn Alan

algate at least

allas alas

alle all

allye (inf. *allyen*) marry

almoost almost

als (N) as

also also; *also . . . as* as . . . as

alswa (N) also

alwey always

amendement amends

amounteth (inf. *amounten*) amounts to

ano(o)n at once

answerd (inf. *answeren*) answered

appul apple

ar (inf. *been*) are

argument argument; disputation, debate (see note on l. 269)

aright the right way

array clothes, gear

art artfulness; (knowledge of) the arts (see note on l. 146)

as as; as if; like

aslepe asleep

asshen ashes

atanes (N) at once

aton united

atte at the, of the

auncetrye (noble) ancestry

auntre (inf. *auntren*) risk

auntred (inf. *auntren*) (l. 351) *auntred him* took the risk

avaunting boasting

avise (inf. *avisen*) *avise thee* consider

avised (inf. *avisen*) see note on l. 479

awak (inf. *awaken*) wake up

away away; gone

awen (N) own

a-werk at work, to work

ay always

ayeyn again; back

baar (inf. *beren*) carried

bad (inf. *bidden*) ordered, told to

bak back

bakward backwards

Glossary

balke beam
banes (N) bones
bar (inf. *beren*) bore
bathe (N) both
Bayard name for a bay-coloured horse
be (inf. *been*) be; (ind. pl.) are; (subjunctive) is, are
bed(de) bed
beddes bed's
bee (inf. *been*) be
been be; are
beest beast, animal
beete (l. 73) (inf. *be(e)ten*) repair
beete (l. 454) (inf. *beten*) beat
ben be; are
benedicite bless me
berd beard; *make a clerkes berd* see note on l. 242
berye berry
beste best; *atte beste* of the best (quality)
bet better
bette (inf. *beten*) beat
bettre better
bibbed (inf. *bibben*) imbibed
bide (inf. *biden*) wait, stay
biforn before; in front of; previously
bigan (inf. *biginnen*) began
bigile (inf. *bigilen*) deceive
bigiled (inf. *bigilen*) deceived
biginne (inf. *biginnen*) begin
bihinde behind
binethe beneath, underneath
bisemare scorn
bisily eagerly, anxiously
bisoght (inf. *bisechen*) besought, begged

bistowe (inf. *bistowen*) bestow, give in marriage
bithoghte (inf. *bithinken*) *him bithoghte* happened to think of
bitwixe between
blake black
blere (inf. *bleren*) deceive
blering deception, hoodwinking
blody bloody
blood blood; family
boes (N) behoves; *him boes* he must
boidekin dagger
bokeler small shield
bolt see *upright*
bood (inf. *biden*) stayed; dwelt
boold bold
boond (inf. *binden*) tied up
boost boast; *craketh boost* see *craketh*
bore (inf. *beren*) born
bounden (inf. *binden*) bound, wound
bras brass
breed bread
bren bran
brest breast, chest
brestes breasts
breyde (inf. *breyden*) awoke
bribe (inf. *briben*) steal
bridale wedding-feast
bridel bridle
brigge bridge
brode broad
Bromeholm Bromholm
brood broad
broun see note on l. 514
burdon refrain

busshel bushel (8 gallons or about 36 litres)

but but; unless; except; only; *but if* unless

buttokes buttocks

by by; alongside; *by and by* side by side

cacche (inf. *cacchen*) catch

cake large flat loaf

cam (inf. *comen*) came

camus snub

Cantebregge, Cantebrigge Cambridge

capul (N) horse

carie (inf. *carien*) carry

carpenteer carpenter

carpenteris carpenter's

cas adventure

caste (inf. *casten*) cast; put; throw; threw

catel property

cause cause; *by cause that* because

chaffare trading

chalons blankets

chambre bedroom

cheere (l. 278) *make us cheere* give us a warm welcome; (l. 509) *made cheere* behaved cheerfully

Chepe Cheapside

cherles peasant's (see note on l. 63)

chidde (inf. *chiden*) complained

chimbe (noun) rim

chimbe (inf. *chimben*) chime

chirche church

chirches church's

citee city

clawed (inf. *clawen*) scratched

cleped (inf. *clepen*) called

clepen call

clerk student; scholar; cleric (see note on l. 164, and Appendix to *An Introduction to Chaucer*)

clerkes students; (l. 174) the learned

cok cock

cokenay milksop, cissy

collegge college

coltes tooth see note on l. 34

compaignye company; (l. 313) *par compaignye* for company's sake

compeer comrade, pal

complin compline, evening service

comth (inf. *comen*) comes

conclusion outcome

contenance appearance

convertible synonymous

coold cold

coppes cups

counte (inf. *counten*) care; value at

coveitise covetousness

cradel cradle

craft trade; (l. 512) gild of tradesmen

craketh (inf. *craken*) cracks; *craketh boost* talks loudly

creep (inf. *crepen*) crept

crekes tricks

crepte (inf. *crepen*) crept (in)

crie (inf. *crien*) shout, cry out

Cristes Christ's

crois cross

cropen (inf. *crepen*) crept

croun crown; head; tonsure

crowke jug

crye (inf. *crien*) cry out; (l. 152)
  crye upon entreat
curs curse
curteisly courteously;
  discreetly
Cutberd Cuthbert
daf (N) fool
dame lady
daunced (inf. *dauncen*) danced
dauncen dance
dawe (inf. *dawen*) dawn
daweninge dawn
deed dead
deere dear
deeth death
degre rank
departen part
depe deep
Depeford Deptford
derk dark
despended (inf. *despenden*)
  spent
despitously cruelly
devel devil
devise (inf. *devisen*) describe,
  relate
devoure (inf. *devouren*) devour,
  swallow up
deynous scornful
dich ditch
dide (inf. *do(o)n*) did
digne disdainful
dignitee excellence
disparage dishonour
dispense spending
disport amusement
doghter daughter
doon do, act; done
dooth (inf. *do(o)n*) does
dore door
dorste (inf. *durren*) dared (to)

dotage senile folly
doun down
doute doubt; *out of doute*
  without doubt
draf-sak sack of draff (see note
  on l. 352)
drede (inf. *dreden*) fear, be
  afraid (of)
drinken drink
drive (inf. *driven*) driven
dronke(n) drunk
drough (inf. *drawen*) drew,
  pulled out
drow (inf. *drawen*) drew
dwale sleeping draught
dwelten (inf. *dwellen*) dwelt,
  lived
dys dice
eek also
eelde old age
elles else
entree entrance
eny any
er (*that*) before
erly early
ese refreshment
esement alleviation, redress
espie (inf. *espien*) notice
estaat rank, position
estres interior
eten (inf. *eten*) eaten
evere ever, always; *evere in*
  oon continually
everemo always, all the time
everideel completely
eyen eyes
fader father; father's
faillen fail
fair(e) beautiful; fine; (ll. 208,
  286) neatly; (l. 215) properly;
  (l. 274) cleverly

Glossary

fal fall

falle (inf. *fallen*) fallen

falles (inf. *fallen*) falls·

fals false, dishonest, deceptive

far(e) (inf. *faren*) behave; go; *fare the wors* (*of*) are the worse (for); *fare we* it fares with us; *fare weel* farewell; *hou fares* how are things with; *I fare* it fares with me, I behave

fare (noun) fuss

fareth (inf. *faren*) *so fareth it* so it is

fay faith

feend devil

feir beautiful

felawe fellow; comrade

felawes companions (see note on l. 258)

fer far

ferly (N) extraordinary

fest fist

fetisly neatly

fey faith

fil (inf. *fallen*) fell; occurred

fint (inf. *finden*) finds

fisshe (inf. *fisshen*) fish

fit spell, time; bout

flour flour; best

flye fly

fnorteth (inf. *fnorten*) snorts

folie folly, foolishness

fond (inf. *finden*) found, discovered

fonne (N) fool

foond (inf. *finden*) found

foot feet

for for, because, on account of; *for that* in order that; *for to* to; *for which* for which

reason; *as for* in return for; *what for* what with

forage dry winter food for cattle

forbede (inf. *forbeden*) forbid

forgat (inf. *forgetten*) forgot

forth forward, on

forther further

forthy therefore

foule badly

fra (N) from

free generous

fro from

ful (adj.) full; (adv.) very

fulle; atte fulle to the fullest extent, in full, as hard as possible

furlong 220 yards (203 metres)

fyr fire

ga (N) go

gadered (inf. *gaderen*) gathered, collected

gaillard cheerful, merry

game joke

gan (inf. *ginnen*) began

gas (N) goes

geen (N) gone

gentil noble

gere equipment

gete (inf. *geten*) get

gif if

gilour deceiver

ginneth (inf. *ginnen*) begins

gise habit

giterne a zither-like instrument

glas glass

gleedes live coals

Goddes God's

good goods, property

gon (inf.) go; run; (past part.) gone

Glossary

goon (inf. *go(o)n*) gone
goos goose
gooth (inf. *go(o)n*) goes; runs
goth (inf. *go(o)n*) goes
gras grass
graspeth (inf. *graspen*) gropes
graunte grant
greet great
grene green
Grenewich Greenwich
grete great
gretteste greatest
greve (inf. *greven*); (l. 5) *him greve*, (l. 56) *yow greve* take offence
greythen (inf. *greythen*) prepare; *greythen hem* get ready
grucche (inf. *grucchen*) grumble
gyde guide
gyte (?)robe
hadde (inf. *ha(ve)n*) had
hail; al hail (N) greetings
halde (N) considered
half-wey halfway through
halle hall, college
halydayes holy days
ham (N) home
han (inf. *ha(ve)n*) have
happed (inf. *happen*) occurred
hardily boldly
hardy bold
harlot rascal, villain
harrow! help!
hast? (inf. *ha(ve)n*) have you?
hastow (inf. *ha(ve)n*) you have
hath (inf. *ha(ve)n*) has
haukes hawks
haunteth (inf. *haunten*) is addicted to

hee he
heed head
heeld (inf. *holden*) held, kept
heelp (inf. *helpen*) helped
heer (noun) hair
heer(e) (inf. *he(e)ren*) hear
heer(e) (adv.) here
heighe high
hem them
hende courteous; handy (see note on l. 2)
henne hence, away
hente (inf. *henten*) seized, took
herbergage lodgings
herberwe lodging
herberwinge giving lodgings
herd(e) (inf. *heren*) heard
herdestow? (inf. *heren*) have you heard?
heris hairs
herkned (inf. *herknen*) listened to
Herry Harry
herte heart
hething (N) contempt
heythen (N) hence
highte (inf. *hoten*) was called
hir(e) her; their
hirselve herself
Hogge Hodge (familiar form of Roger)
hoker disdain
homwarde homeward
hond hand
honoure (inf. *honouren*) honour, confer honour on
hony honey
hooly holy
hoor hoary, white
hoord store
Hoost(e) host

120

Glossary

hoote hot, fiery
hope (inf. *hopen*) expect
hoppe(n) (inf. *hoppen*) dance
hopur hopper (see note on l. 182)
hors horse
hose(n) stockings
hostileer innkeeper
hous house
housbondrie management, economy
howgates (N) how
howve hood; *sette his howve* make a fool of him
hye high; grandly
ik (N) I
il (N) bad
ilhail (N) bad luck
ilke same
ille (N) poor
in in; on
inne in
inward in, indoors
ire anger
is (N) am
Jakke Jack (see note on l. 493)
jalous jealous
Jame James
jape trick, joke
jay jay (bird)
jolily merrily
joly pretty; merry
jolyf merry
jossa! down here!
kamus snub
kan (inf. *konnen*) can; know how to
keep (noun) care
keep! (inf. *kepen*) keep still!
kepe (inf. *kepen*) keep, protect; watch for

kin kindred, family, relations
kinrede kindred, (grand) relations
knede (inf. *kneden*) knead
knit (inf. *knitten*) fastened
knyf knife
konne (inf. *konnen*) can; know how to
koude (inf. *konnen*) could; knew how to
lad (inf. *leden*) led, taken
langage manner of speech
lange (N) long
lasse less
laste last
lat (inf. *letten*) let
laten blode bled (see note on l. 492)
lathe (N) barn
laughen (inf. *laughen*) laughed
laus loose
layth (inf. *layen*, *leyen*) lays, puts
leche doctor
leep (inf. *lepen*) leapt
leet (inf. *leten*) gave up, ceased; let
legge (inf. *leggen*) lay
leith (inf. *layen*, *leyen*) lays; *leith on* lays on, attacks
lemes limbs
lemman sweetheart
lenger longer; *ever lenger* continually
lepe (inf. *lepen*) leap, rush
lepinge leaping
lerned (inf. *lernen*) learnt
lete (inf. *leten*) let
leve (inf. *leven*) leave off
leve (noun) leave, permission, dismissal

Glossary

leveful permissible
levesel leafy shelter
leye (inf. *layen*, *leyen*) lay, wager
lif life
light light; (l. 300) cheerful
lightly easily
linage lineage, descent
list(e) (no inf.) it pleases, it pleased
lite(l) little
lith (inf. *lien*) lies
lokkes (locks of) hair
Londoun London
longen belong, appertain
lo(o)! see!
looketh (inf. *looken*) looks
loos loose
lorn (inf. *lesen*) lost
los loss
lough(e) (inf. *laughen*) laughed
lovede (inf. *loven*) loved
lowke accomplice, decoy
lusty vigorous, eager
lyf life
magestee majesty
maide virgin
maister master
maken make
maketh (inf. *maken*) makes, gets
maladye illness; *on a maladye* in an illness
Malyne see note on l. 382
man man; (l. 275) one
manciple see *maunciple*
mariage marriage
market-betere loafer around markets
maunciple manciple, provisions officer

meete (inf. *meeten*) meet
mele meal
melle mill
melodye melody
men people
meschaunce ill luck
mesuage dwelling-house with land
mete food
meynee company, gang
might power, potency
mighte (no inf.) might, could
mille mill
millere miller
milleris miller's
mine my, mine
minstralcye minstrelsy, jollification
mirthe high spirits
misgo(o)(n) (inf. *misgo(o)n*) gone astray
mo more
moore more
moot (no inf.) must; may
mote (no inf.) may
mowe (no inf.) may
mowled (inf. *mowlen*) decayed
mullok rubbish-heap
myn my, mine
myrie merry, good-humoured, pleasant
na (N) no
nafors (N) no matter, nevertheless
nam (inf. *be(e)n*) am not
nameliche especially, in particular
namely especially, in particular
namoore no more
nas (inf. *be(e)n*) was not
nat not

Glossary

nathelees nevertheless
nay denial
ne nor; not
nede necessity
nedede (inf. *neden*) needed,
  was necessary; *hem nedede*
  they needed
nedes business, affairs
neen (N) no
neer nearer
nekke neck(s)
nettes (fishing-)nets
Newegate Newgate prison
nice foolish
nicetee foolishness
nis (inf. *be(e)n*) is not
niste (inf. *witen*) did not know
noble splendid
noght not
nonnerye nunnery
noon none; no-one; nothing
nortelrie education
note business
ny near; nearly
o one
of along; at; by; from; of; off
of-showve (inf. *of-showven*)
  repel
oghte (inf. *owen*) ought
oold old
oon one; (l. 436) someone; *in
  oon* see *evere*
oonly only, simply
oother second; other
open-ers medlar
Osewold Oswald
owene own
pace (inf. *passen*) go; pace
page boy, lad
paire pair
palfrey small horse

panade long knife, cutlass
panne pan
papir paper(s), accounts
paramour romance
parte (inf. *parten*) part
pastee pasty, meat-pie
payed (inf. *payen*) paid
payen pay
pecock peacock
peer equal
peert bold
peny penny; payment
peraventure perhaps
percely parsley
perilous dangerous, aggressive
Perkin Pete
person parson, parish-priest
peyne pain, suffering
philosophye philosophy;
  learning
pigges piglets
piled bald
pipen pipe, play the pipe(s)
pit (N) put
pley (noun) jest, joke
pleyde (inf. *pleyen*) (l. 4) were
  amused; (l. 214) amused
  himself
pley(e) (inf. *pleyen*) amuse
  oneself, enjoy oneself, joke
pleyen play
pleyneth (inf. *pleynen*) laments
point detail, respect
poke bag, small sack
poppere dagger
pose cold
povre poor
preche (inf. *prechen*) preach
prentis apprentice
prentishood apprenticeship
priketh (inf. *priken*) thrusts

123

Glossary

prime see note on l. 52
prively secretly
privetee privacy; private dwelling
propre fine
purpos purpose, intention
pye magpie
quaad bad
quakke hoarseness
queynte ingenious
quit (inf. *quiten*) repaid
quite (inf. *quiten*) repay
quod (inf. *quethen*) said
raa (N) roe deer
rage (inf. *ragen*) flirt
redy ready
reed red
rein rain
reine rein
releved (inf. *releven*) granted remedy
remenaunt remainder
ren run
renne(n) (inf. *rennen*) run
reve reeve (see Introduction, p. 26)
reve (inf. *reven*) rob
revel merry-making
revelour merry-maker; merry-making
revelrye gaiety
ribaudye coarseness, filth
ribible a kind of lute or fiddle
riding procession
right just, exactly, truly
riot dissipation
riote (inf. *rioten*) live in debauchery
riotous dissipated
rist (inf. *risen*) rises
rokken rock

roos (inf. *risen*) rose
rosted (inf. *rosten*) roasted
roten (inf. *roten*) rotten
rotie (inf. *rotien*) rot, cause to rot
roum roomy
routhe pity; lamentation
rowmer roomier
rowteth (inf. *rowten*) snores
rowting snoring
sak sack
sakked (inf. *sakken*) put in sacks
sal (N) shall; must
sale (N) soul
Salomon Solomon
sang (N) song
saugh (inf. *seen*) saw
saule soul
save except (for)
saven preserve
savinge excepting
sayn (inf. *say(e)n*) say
scape escape
scolers scholars
se (inf. *seen*) see
seel happiness; salvation
seen see
seid(e) (inf. *sey(e)n*) said, told
seint saint
seist (inf. *sey(e)n*) sayest, say
seith (inf. *sey(e)n*) says
sely wretched
sende (inf. *senden*) sent
sermoning preaching
servaunt servant, employee
sette (inf. *setten*) set; *sette his howvve* see *howvve*; *sette a tare* see *tare*
setten (inf. *setten*) *setten stevene* made an appointment

Glossary

sey(e) (inf. *sey(e)n*) say, tell, speak

seyn say, tell, speak

shawe wood

sheete (inf. *she(e)ten*) shoot (with bow and arrow)

Sheffeld Sheffield

shende (inf. *shenden*) ruin, spoil

shimering glimmer

shipman sailor

sholde (inf. *shullen*) should, had to, was going to, ought to

shoon (inf. *shinen*) shone

shoppe shop, workplace

shortly briefly

shrewe scoundrel

shul (inf. *shullen*) must, shall

sik sick, ill

sikerly certainly, for certain

Simond Simon

sin (that) since

sire father

sires (ladies and) gentlemen

sithe since

sitteth (inf. *sitten*) sits; reigns

sleighte cunning

slepestow? (inf. *slepen*) are you asleep?

slik (N) such

smale small

smoot (inf. *smiten*) hit, punched

smoterlich sullied

snibbed (inf. *snibben*) rebuked, scolded

softe(ly) quietly

soghte (inf. *sechen*) was looking for, through

sokene custom (see note on l. 133)

solace (inf. *solacen*) entertain

Soler see note on l. 136

som some

somde(e)l somewhat

somtime sometimes, occasionally

somwhat something

soold (inf. *sellen*) sold

soore fiercely

sooth true; truly; truth

soper supper

sorwe sorrow

sothe; for sothe in truth

sothly truly

soupen eaten supper

soutere cobbler

sowke (inf. *sowken*) suck, breast-feed; (l. 562) extract (money)

spak (inf. *speken*) spoke, was speaking

spare (inf. *sparen*) defer to

sparkles small sparks

speche speech, words

sped (inf. *speden*) prospered, been successful

spede (inf. *speden*) hasten

speke (inf. *speken*) speak, talk

speketh (inf. *speken*) speaks

sporned (inf. *spornen*) stumbled

staf stick

stal (inf. *stelen*) stole

stalk piece of straw, 'mote'

stand! (inf. *standen*) stand still!

stele (inf. *stelen*) steal

stevene appointment

stide stead, place

stiketh (inf. *stiken*) sticks, is fastened

stinte (inf. *stinten*) stop, cease

Glossary

stirte (inf. *stirten*) started, leapt

stoln (inf. *stelen*) stolen

stoon stone

stounde while, period; (l. 138) see note

straunge difficult; *straunge he made it of* he made difficulties about

stree straw

streem stream

streit narrow

strepeth (inf. *strippen*) strips

stryf strife, struggle

stubbel (fed on) stubble

suffise (inf. *suffisen*) be sufficient

sustenance support

swa (N) so

swain (N) servant

swerd sword

swich such; *swich a* a certain

swilk (N) such

swink labour, exertion

swonken (inf. *swinken*) laboured

swoor (inf. *sweren*) swore

swyve (inf. *swyven*) have sexual intercourse (with)

swyved (inf. *swyven*) had sexual intercourse with, enjoyed sexually

taa (N) take

tail tail; behind; sexual parts

take (inf. *taken*) taken

tald (N) told, related

tappe tap; bung; bunghole

tare weed; (l. 146) *sette a tare*, (l. 202) *counte a tare* care a scrap

tarie (inf. *tarien*) waste

termes terms

testif headstrong

thair (N) their

than then; than

thanne then

thar (no inf.) it is necessary; (l. 466) *him thar* he ought, needs

that that, who

thee you, yourself

theef thief

theek (N) I prosper

thefte theft

thenne (l. 212) thin

ther there; where; *ther as* where

therbiforn before that

therfore therefore

therof about that

therto moreover

therwithal with that

thider thither, to it

thikke thick; plump

thise these

thogh though

thoghte (inf. *thinken*) thought

though that though, even though

thoughte (inf. *thinken*) it seemed

thridde third

thries thrice, three times

thrift prosperity; *by my thrift* as I hope to prosper

throte-bolle Adam's apple

thurgh through

thwitel large knife

thyn your

tides (N) betides

til (that) till, until

til (N) (ll. 185, 256) to

time time(s); (l. 204) opportunity

126

Glossary

tipet see note on l. 99

tobreke (inf. *tobreken*) break apart

tobroke (inf. *tobreken*) smashed in

tonge tongue

tonne barrel

toty dizzy

toun(e) settlement, village, town

traitour betrayer, deceiver

trenchant cutting, sharp

trewely truly, honestly

trouthe honesty

trowe (inf. *trowen*) believe

Trumpingtoun Trumpington

tulle (inf. *tullen*) entice, attract

turne (inf. *turnen*) turn (on a lathe)

twa (N) two

twies twice

unhardy cowardly

unseely unfortunate

unthank curse

unto to

unweelde feeble

upright(e) supine, on her back; *bolt upright* flat on her back

usaunt accustomed, addicted

vernisshed (inf. *vernisshen*) varnished (see note on l. 295)

verray true, genuine; completely

vileynye injury

vitailliers victuallers, keepers of inns or eating-houses

volupeer night-cap

vouchesauf (inf. *vouchen sauf*) grant, agree

waat (N) knows

wagges (inf. *waggen*) shakes

waked (inf. *waken*) stayed awake

wal(les) wall(s)

walwe (inf. *walwen*) roll about

wanges (N) back teeth

warderere! look out behind!

wardeyn warden, head of college

wasten use up, consume

wax (inf. *waxen*) grew

weel well

weet wet

wel well; easily; much; (l. 520) *wel was* it was well with

wenche girl

wende(n) (inf. *wenen*) supposed, imagined, thought

wendest (inf. *wenden*) go

wene (inf. *wenen*) suppose, imagine, expect

wepe (inf. *wepen*) weep

were (inf. *be(e)n*) were; (l. 54) would be

wered (inf. *weren*) worn

werkes (inf. *werken*) ache

wers worse

wery weary

wey(e) way

weylaway! alas!

wha (N) who

whan (that) when

what what; (l. 48) why

wher where; *wher so* wherever

whete wheat

whil (that) while, as long as

whilk (N) which

whilom formerly, once

wight (adj.) (N) swift

Glossary

wight (noun) person, creature; (l. 429) *lite wight* little bit

wikked wicked, evil

wil (inf. *willen*) will

wil (noun) will, desire

wile trick, stratagem

wiltow will you

wisly certainly, for certain

wiste (inf. *witen*) knew

wit wisdom

withinne within

withouten without

wo woe, sorrow

wol (inf. *willen*) will, want to

wolde (inf. *willen*) would; wished for

wombe belly

woot (inf. *witen*) know

worthy respectable

wrang (N) wrong(ly)

wrecchednesse miserable or sinful behaviour

writeth (inf. *writen*) declares, indicates

wro(o)th(e) angry; (l. 544) at variance, incompatible

wyf wife

yaf (inf. *yeven*) gave

ybake (inf. *baken*) baked

ybete (inf. *beten*) beaten

ybounde (inf. *binden*) tied up

ycomen (inf. *comen*) come; *ycomen of* descended from

ye (interjection) (monosyllabic) yes

ye (noun) (disyllabic) eye

ye (pronoun) (monosyllabic) you

yeer year(s)

yeris years

yet still, yet, moreover

yeve (inf. *yeven*) give, grant

yexeth (inf. *yexen*) hiccoughs

yfaith in faith, indeed

yfostred (inf. *fostren*) brought up, educated

ygrounde (inf. *grinden*) ground

ygrowen (inf. *growen*) grown

yit yet

ykembd (inf. *kemben*) combed

ylaft (inf. *leven*) left

ylost (inf. *lesen*) lost

ymaked (inf. *maken*) made

ymel (N) among

ynorissed (inf. *norissen*) brought up, nurtured

yomanrye (l. 95) *of yomanrye* as a yeoman

yon (N) yonder, that

yonge young

yoore long ago

yow you; yourself, yourselves

yreke (inf. *raken*) raked

yronne (inf. *rennen*) run

yset (inf. *setten*) set

yseyn (inf. *seen*) seen

yshapen (inf. *shapen*) provided

ysped (inf. *speden*) prospered

yspred (inf. *spreden*) spread

ytoold (inf. *tellen*) told

yvele evil

ywet (inf. *wetten*) wet

ywis indeed